100 SKILLS

You'll Need for the
END OF THE WORLD
WORLD
(AS WE KNOW IT)

ANA MARIA SPAGNA

Illustrations by Brian Cronin

D0962994

Storey Publishing

*The mission of Storey Publishing is to serve our customers by
publishing practical information that encourages
personal independence in harmony with the environment.*

Edited by Deborah Burns
Art direction and design by Alethea Morrison

Cover and interior illustrations by © Brian Cronin,
 except: Alethea Morrison, 16–17, 76–77, 124–125, 134–135, 180–181;
 Bethany Caskey, 118 (bottom three), 119; Beverly Duncan, 88 (top and
 bottom left), 89 (top left); Brigita Fuhrmann, 118 (top six); Charles Joslin,
 88 (bottom right); Kimberly Knauf, 24–25; Sarah Brill, 88 (top right), 89
 (all but top left)
Hand lettering throughout by Alethea Morrison

 Storey books are available for special premium and promotional
uses and for customized editions. For further information, please call
1-800-793-9396.

Storey Publishing
210 MASS MoCA Way
North Adams, MA 01247
www.storey.com

Printed in the United States by Versa Press
10 9 8 7 6 5 4 3 2 1

LIBRARY OF CONGRESS CATALOGING-IN-PUBLICATION DATA ON FILE.

Ten of the ideas in this book appeared in "10 Skills to Hone for a Post-Oil
Future" by Ana Maria Spagna, *Orion*, Vol. 32, No. 3 (May/June 2013).

CONTENTS

FUTURE TENSE

IN MY FIRST CLASS AS A HIGH SCHOOL FRESHMAN, I entered the room to find every inch of every blackboard covered with numbers. Huh? The teacher, a biblical scholar, tried to get us to guess what the numbers were. Lottery numbers? Algebraic formulas? Secret codes? No. They were dates, we could tell that much, but for what?

Eventually he explained that these were all dates on which someone, likely a prophet, had predicted that the world would end. Since then, we've survived a predicted apocalypse a few times, from midnight 1999 to the 2012 Mayan calendar deadline, and so far we're safe.

One thing is certain: we don't know when or if the world will end. But we also don't know what the future may bring, and we can't expect things to stay exactly as they are. The possibility that catastrophic changes wrought by war or disease or a random meteor strike or, most urgently, climate change will come in our lifetime seems very real. As does the possibility that such changes — or efforts to avoid them — will require us to live closer to the land, closer to one another, and farther from our touch screens and shiny, fast vehicles.

There are plenty of ways to plan for an uncertain future from political or philosophical or religious standpoints, but what about practical ways? Some of the skills in this book take from the past (blacksmithing, wheel building, tinkering). Many others are practiced today as occupations (barbering, welding, home childbirth) or as hobbies (music making, knitting, sailing). Several of the skills are no-brainers; it comes down to basic survival (planting, foraging, shelter building, water collecting). Others might not seem as obvious but may be more crucial. Skills like listening, negotiating, borrowing, and bartering will be as essential in radically changed times as they are now. The most important skills may be those that require us to rethink the familiar, to adopt a new perspective (daydreaming, porch sitting, revising).

No one will master all these skills. But anyone can tinker in several and practice a few seriously. You probably do already. Just thinking about the rest can spur insight and debate. You'll undoubtedly think of skills we overlooked. Start your own list. Keep it running. You never know when you'll need it.

1

ANIMAL HUSBANDRY

RAISE CHICKENS FOR EGGS, sheep for wool, cows for milk, horses to ride, oxen for work, pigeons for sending messages. Commit to their care. You'll need to build shelters, grow or procure food for them, protect them from predators and disease, breed them and birth them, deal with their injuries and their waste. You can't leave them to go on a walkabout or a hunting trip or to visit relatives. (See also: *Staying Home.*)

You can read about raising animals the way expectant parents read about raising children, for months or years, but you won't know what you're in for until the little live things arrive in your care. Then it's all you. Give them good, clean water, manure-free pens, a low-stress environment. The benefits may take years to accrue. The joy of companionship starts right away.

◆ ◆ ◆

2

BARBERING

ANYONE WHO'S TRIED TO CUT HAIR with a Swiss Army knife and a mirror can tell you: it takes some expertise. To barber well requires a combination of fine motor skills, aesthetic vision, and, yes, communication skills, since you won't be cutting just your own hair, not anymore. Barbering is a universal need and, therefore, a valuable skill to barter. Get good scissors and keep them sharp. Carry them with you everywhere. You never know when someone might need a trim.

Some tips:

» Keep your scissors level as you cut. Cross-check often to ensure that sides are even.

» For a very short cut, try moving a comb across the head at a slightly tipped angle and clipping straight along the tine edge.

» Learn to use a straight razor to give a close shave. Keep the strop handy, and remember to sterilize between uses. An occasional nick is inevitable.

3

BARTERING

BABY CLOTHES FOR BOOTS. Extra vegetables for a fresh-caught trout. Wood-splitting for homebrew. Bread-baking for rent. Advice for a cup of tea.

Bartering doesn't always come out even. Piano lessons might be worth more than ditchdigging. Or vice versa. Horseshoeing is more dangerous than haircutting. Usually. At some point you quit keeping track.

There are a thousand ways to acquire what you need without money . . . and to give it away, too.

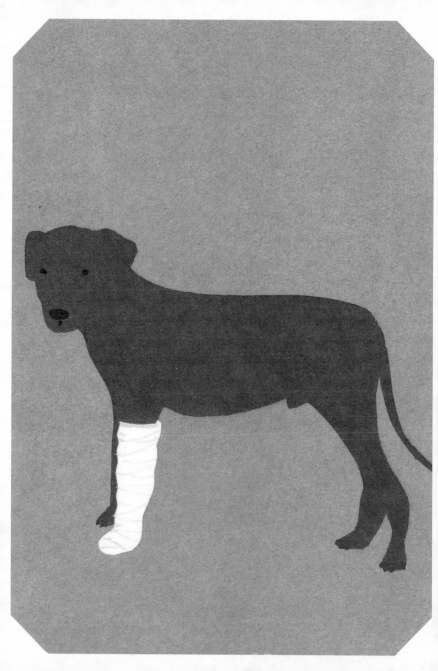

4

BASIC FIRST AID

IT STARTS WITH KNOWLEDGE: What's the difference between heat stroke and heat exhaustion? When do you give a diabetic sugar? What are the symptoms of stroke versus shock? Your response moves toward pragmatism. Encourage rest and water. Administer medicine if you have it — insulin, epinephrine, ibuprofen. Take critical steps as necessary: start CPR, say, or stitch a wound.

Here's how to do the latter. First clean the wound with boiled water and soap. Sterilize the needle (and thread), stick it in at a 90-degree angle, and poke hard; even thin skin is thicker than we think. Silk is easiest, or nylon, but any thread will work. Keep the stitches a quarter inch apart and the same distance from the edge of the wound.

If the wound is long, you can tie off your thread with a square knot between stitches to avoid slippage. Avoid puckering. Tie a square knot again at the end. Nothing to it. You don't have to be Rambo.

Remember: First, do no harm.
Then balance that with this: What if you do nothing at all?

BASIC BANDAGING

Making a Bandage

3 feet

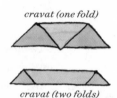

triangular bandage

cravat (one fold)

cravat (two folds)

Bandaging a Palm

Bandaging a Hand

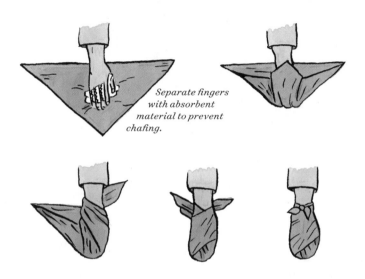

Separate fingers with absorbent material to prevent chafing.

Bandaging an Elbow

5

BEEKEEPING

HONEY BEES HAVE HAD A ROUGH GO OF IT LATELY. Colony collapse disorder has killed off millions of hives in the past decade. And what's bad for the bees is bad for us all. Last year, as a demonstration, one Whole Foods store removed all the items that depend on honey bees and other pollinators; the produce section was half empty.

If you want to start your own hives, the American Beekeeping Federation provides free beginner information. If you're not up for building boxes, you can easily accommodate pollinating passersby. About 70 percent of native bees nest in the ground, alone, not in colonies: mason bees, mining bees, sweat bees. To make them feel at home, all you need is a pile of dirt and sand. Nothing fancy; they shun good soil. Toss some rotting logs across the top and allow grass to grow tall around the sides.

The best alternative may be the bed-and-breakfast approach. Flowers — cosmos, bachelor buttons, sunflowers, poppies — and fruit trees provide great pollinator habitat. Plant them liberally, let wildflowers flourish, and await your guests.

6

BICYCLE REPAIR

BICYCLES ARE THE MOST COMMON VEHICLE on the planet today. They can be refitted to be recumbent or to haul heavy items, humans or otherwise, and there are enough discarded parts to keep us on the roads for a long time. Hoard the parts first: tires and tubes, seats and shifters, brake pads and pedals. Graduate to organizing the parts by cable gauge and wheel rim size.

After that, bicycle repair is all about practice. Start with fixing a flat or oiling a rusty chain and move up to spoking a wheel, repacking bearings, replacing a derailleur.

Improvise as necessary. (See also: *Tinkering.*)

———◆◆◆———

7

BIRD LISTENING

WHAT'S THE BEST INDICATOR OF DANGER approaching? The animals know. Birds sound the alarm, and the rest of the creatures take cover. And not just danger — birds can herald a change in weather or the arrival of long-awaited guests or help. Listening to them takes training in discernment. Note which birds visit your region in which season and which habitat (forest, swamp, orchard, river?), and learn their repertoire of calls. A bird call might be metallic or musical, a whinny or a whistle, a rattle or a caw or a trill, or, as with the mockingbird, all of the above.

More to the point, birds vocalize to serve different purposes — there's the social call, injury call, courtship song. To recognize an alarm, listen for a ruckus and then look around for the cause. A predator bird, a hawk, or an owl? A weather event? An approaching stranger? Next time you'll know better what to expect.

Note: Birds give false alarms. With practice, you'll learn that, as with an injured toddler, some cries are for show and some mean business.

◆ ◆

MNEMONIC BIRD SONGS

To help identify bird songs, listeners have devised phrases mimicking them. These phrases are known as mnemonics — tricks designed to aid the memory.

YELLOW WARBLER
"Sweet, sweet, little more sweet"

AMERICAN GOLDFINCH
"Potato-chip" (often in flight)

HERMIT THRUSH
"Why don't you come to me"

COMMON YELLOWTHROAT
"Witchety, witchety, witchety"

INDIGO BUNTING
"Fire, fire! Where, where? Here, here"

SONG SPARROW
"Maids, maids, maids, put on the teakettle-ettle-ettle"

AMERICAN ROBIN
"Cheer up, cheerily, cheer up"

RED-TAILED HAWK
"Ski-errr!" (often in flight)

BLACK-CAPPED CHICKADEE
"Hey, sweetie"
"Chickadee-dee-dee"

RED-WINGED BLACKBIRD
"Konk-la-reee"

NORTHERN CARDINAL
"Purdy, purdy, purdy"

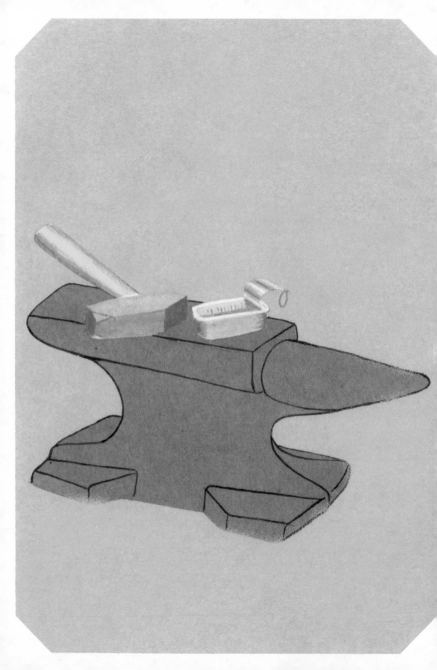

8

BLACKSMITHING

TO LEARN HOW TO LIVE in a post-industrial world, consider the pre-industrial world where blacksmiths made everything: tools, nails, hinges, lamps, hooks, horseshoes, gates, and railings. Wheels, even! Think of all the discarded steel we'll have. A blacksmith could turn basketball rims to fish spears, house gutters to sleigh runners, rusted car panels to cookware.

Take a class. Find a forge, and an anvil. Build a fire, and your forearms.

9

BORROWING & *LENDING*

EASIER SAID THAN DONE. Borrowing means admitting you have needs you can't fill on your own. Pride gets in the way; so does fear. Borrowing also means taking the time to ask. That guy down the road, the one with every tool imaginable? He'll talk your ear off for an hour before he hands over the square-bit driver. Borrowing, finally, means taking responsibility. Sharpen the pruners before you give them back, pre-thread the needles in the sewing kit, clean the food dehydrator screens.

Then there's lending. Letting others use what's yours can have consequences. Lending something hardy like a hammer or a book might be easy enough (depending on the book). Lending stuff that will never come back — a pound of coffee, a growler of beer, a box of apples — might be more difficult (depending on the beer).

Lending possessions that can be easily ruined — a sharp saw, a musical instrument, a bicycle on a muddy day — that's *really* hard. Do it anyhow. Generosity builds community, and community means protection. So let the stuff go.

Also: Lending makes it a whole lot easier to borrow.

10
BRINING

EVER HAD DOLMAS AT A GREEK RESTAURANT? Those delicious stuffed grape leaves? You wouldn't want to chew those leaves pre-brine. Ditto for the olives on the backyard tree in California. Brining — soaking in salt water — is an easier way to preserve food than canning or pickling, and brined foods can be uniquely satisfying. Scientists tell us that humans crave salt because the trace minerals in natural salt allow fluids to pass in and out of cells. Some even suggest that salt is mood elevating.

So those dolmas? Add a pound of kosher salt to a gallon of water. Roll the grape leaves tight and soak them in the solution in a jar with a small stone atop to pack them down. Remove a day before use. Rinse and blanch and stuff. Olives? Bruise them or prick them and stuff them in the same solution. Rinse and replace the brine each day for 12 days. End with cold clean water for 24 hours, and then taste. If too salty, fill with cold water again and wait another day.

◆ ◆ ◆

11

BUTCHERING

YOU NEED A SHARP KNIFE AND A STEADY HAND. Attention to detail and curiosity about how things work are a plus, as is a keen knowledge of anatomy. A strong stomach? Overrated. At some point, you get used to the smell or you ignore it.

The need for meticulous planning, though, cannot be overstated. For large animals, you'll need a block and tackle or a chain and hook or a gambrel to hang them to bleed or cure, plus a bone saw to work through the limbs and a cleaver to split the back bone. For a pig you'll need a scraper, and for a chicken you'll need a plucker, though wadded-up newspaper rubbed vigorously will work.

Immaculate surfaces and utensils, rigorous temperature control, and proper storage can't be improvised. Ignore those details, and you will have a weak stomach indeed.

◆ ◆ ◆

12

CAIRN BUILDING

YOU'VE PROBABLY SEEN THESE STRUCTURES. Spiritual seekers and aspiring artists and bored unlucky anglers stack river rubble in improbable combinations — big flat ones atop small round ones — to create startling sculptures, to symbolize healing, or to delight passersby. That's a fine way to pass the time, but cairns have practical applications, too.

A heap of stones can mark a trail or a property line, a climbing route, or a grave. Whatever your purpose, you want to make your cairn sturdy: the recommendation is three points of contact per rock. You also want it to stand out. Use rocks with colors that contrast with surroundings, light stones against dark forest.

Unless, of course, you don't want it to stand out. Cairns can also be used to show the way to a secret stash — late-season morels or sweet alpine huckleberries — in a way others won't recognize. But you will.

◆ ◆

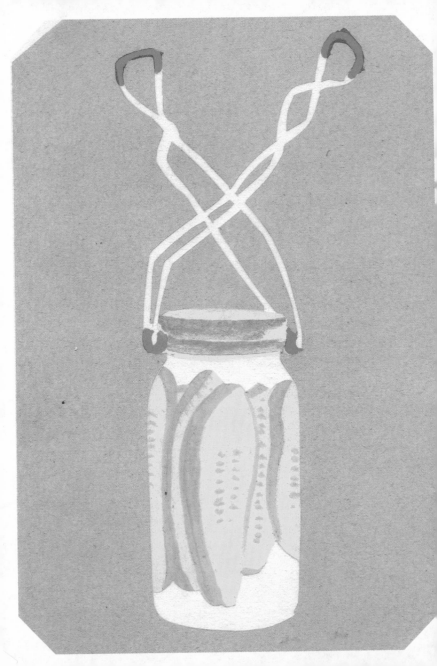

13
CANNING

THE PROBLEM WITH SUMMER'S ABUNDANCE is that it's so abundant. Maybe nothing's better than a home-grown tomato, as Guy Clark sings, but when you have buckets full in the kitchen in September and fruit flies are on the march, you've got a problem. Then, in winter, the problem is the flip side: not enough. So, we can do what our grandparents did: preserve. It's not hard. A glut of how-tos crowd the bookstores, or your friendly state agricultural Extension agent will be glad to help. Here are a few tips.

Clean your jars with very hot water. Use brand-new lids. (See also: *Hoarding.*) Avoid jars with nicked rims. Low-acidity foods require higher temps, even higher than boiling, to prevent botulism, so a pressure cooker is necessary, especially for meat and fish. Use a jar lifter to avoid burns and/or a dropped jar shattering all over the floor.

Listen for the satisfying pop of a lid sealing soon after you remove a jar from the water. For vanity, wipe the cooled and sealed jars with a clean cloth for shiny shelf appearance. For sanity, date and label your jars, and use the oldest first.

◆◆◆

14

CAPTURING ENERGY

MOST POWER THESE DAYS depends on batteries or transmission lines, but there are simpler ways to capture energy. The sun can heat dark pipes or tanks for hot water or, through windows and with insulation, heat your home. A woodstove can do the same where sunlight is scarce. Run pipes through the firebox or wrap them around the stovepipe to heat water via thermosiphon. (Just make sure the tank is higher than the heat source. Remember: heat rises.) Stone, tiles, bricks, or masonry can store heat and mete it out over time.

Running water can power a hydraulic ram pump to move water, or a water wheel to drive belts or gears to mill lumber or make cloth or paper or grind grain. A windmill can do the same where water is scarce.

And wind, water, sun, and fire are just the start. There's methane from cow dung, coffee grounds as fuel pellets, gasification of juniper and mesquite, and plenty more energy sources left for you to imagine. (See also: *Daydreaming.*)

◆ ◆ ◆

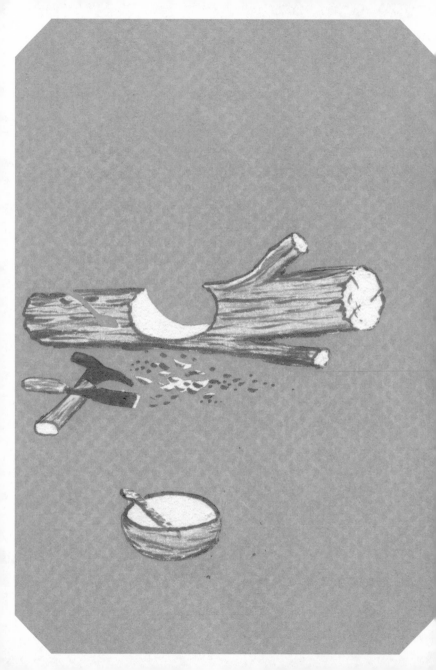

15
CARVING

DEF. 1. *Making or shaping by cutting, chipping, and/or hewing*

Carve a gourd or a burl, a bone or an antler. Carve a spoon or a bowl, a flower vase or a Halloween mask. Carve a roast turkey with care to make sure you get every last morsel. Get even more ambitious and carve a tree to make a dugout canoe, linoleum for prints, a rock for a headstone.

A knife works fine most of the time, but for depth you'll want an adz or a gouge, preferably a whole set. Don't forget the whetstone.

DEF. 2. *Creating a space or a niche for yourself*

Carve out some time to do what's meaningful. Find a place and people you love. Find a purpose, a way to thrive and contribute. No one's going to master all these skills. Find your niche and settle in.

———◆◆———

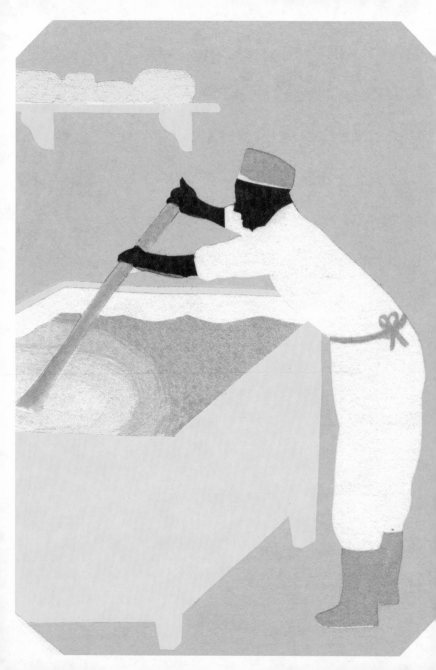

16

CHEESEMAKING

IN THE BEGINNING, nomads stored goat or sheep milk in vessels made from the animals' stomachs. Lactic acid, rennet, and bacteria would ferment the milk and allow it to keep as they traveled long distances. It's not much harder today. You will not need a sheep stomach, but you will need milk. Cow, buffalo, goat, or sheep. The fresher the better. And you will need a culture, usually rennet in liquid or powder form, a thermometer, cheesecloth, and salt.

It's as much art as science, but the gist is simple: heat the milk and watch the temperature, add the culture, let it coagulate, then let it drain through cheesecloth. Salt and finish. (*Note*: Salt adds flavor and also keeps bacteria from forming excessive acid.)

As an easy alternative, try making yogurt. Save some culture from a previous batch, as with sourdough starter, warm the milk and watch the temperature (heat to 176°F, cool to 112°F), add the culture, and wait 6 to 7 hours. Bacteria will do the rest.

◆ ◆ ◆

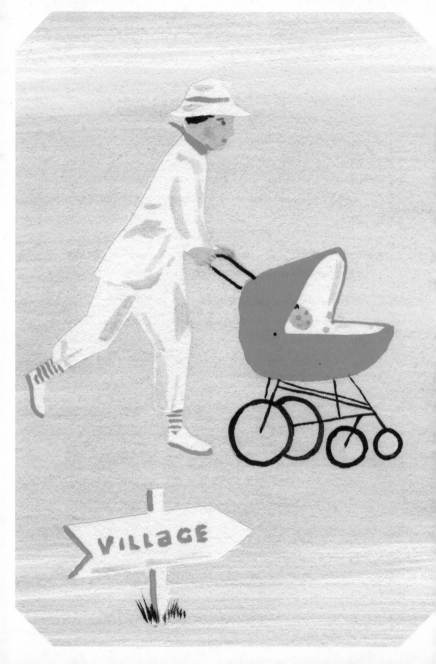

17

CHILD REARING

THERE'S NO HARDER JOB, no more important job, no more rewarding job. You feed them and clothe them and shelter them. You sacrifice sleep, years' worth. You urge them, nag them, beg them, force them to do chores or homework, to clean bedrooms or write thank-you notes, especially when they don't want to. Read to them. Play with them. Teach them to count and to say please. You learn to recognize a fever by a kiss on the forehead, a broken heart by a surly scowl.

Call it what you will: mothering, fathering, aunt-and-uncling, stepparenting, foster parenting, godparenting, grandparenting. Raising children takes patience and diligence and knowledge and wisdom — not least in recognizing when it's time to let go — and sometimes, yes, a village.

The better job we do, the brighter the future looks.

18

CHIMNEY CLEANING

FIRST YOU'LL NEED KNOWLEDGE of creosote, that tarry soot buildup created by wood burned too cool or incompletely. You'll need to learn how green wood and certain tree species, pine especially, create more of it; how creosote is highly flammable; and how a chimney fire can take down a house in less time than it takes to read this page. (See also: *Fire Fighting.*)

Next comes prevention: burn the fire hot; avoid pitchy wood and soft wood; if you have a stovepipe, avoid unnecessary 90-degree bends and add a simple clean-out. Then comes preparation. You'll need eye protection, a dust mask, and gloves; a ladder, a flashlight, a tarp, and old clothes; and a steel brush that fits your chimney.

Finally it's time to choose your approach. You can lower the brush on a chain from the roof, a technique for which you'll need a harness and a penchant for climbing. Or you can push the brush up with sections of stiff wire. It's a dirty job, sometimes dangerous, but someone has to do it, or the consequences can be grave.

◆ ◆

19

CLOUD READING

HOW TO FORECAST WEATHER without satellites or radar? Watch the sky. Cauliflower-like cumulus clouds build before a thunderstorm. High wispy cirrus clouds arrive in advance of a front. A sundog — an eerie circle around the sun on a cloudy day — announces rain-to-come, as does a halo around the moon. Maybe the best way to start is with nautical rhymes. We all know this one.

> *Red sky at night, sailor's delight.*
> *Red sky at morning, sailors take warning.*

Meaning: At mid-latitudes, weather comes from the west. If the sun rising in the east illuminates the high-level clouds, they're coming your way. Conversely, if the sunset illuminates the clouds, they're in the east and heading out. The red itself comes from scattering of sunlight through particulates in the atmosphere. Then there's this one.

> *Mares' tails and mackerel scales*
> *Make lofty ships take in their sails.*

Meaning: As the jet stream breaks up existing patterns, cirrus clouds get elongated into wispy curves like mares' tails, and the altocumulus start to resemble fish scales. Change is on its way.

◆ ◆ ◆

20

COBBLING

DEF. 1. Shoemaking

You'll need a welting awl to stitch the upper to the sole, a sleeking bone to smooth the curves, a rasp to remove burrs. You'll need pliers and a punch, scissors and a knife, hammers, nippers, nail pullers, a heel iron, and a deer bone. You'll need hand strength and a flair for design. Shoemaking is not, as it turns out, at all like Definition 2.

DEF. 2. Putting something together roughly or hastily; assembling from available parts

Cobble together dinner or shelter. Cobble together a Halloween costume. Cobble together a living from a dozen different jobs. Cobbling is flexibility with raw materials, improvisation with rewards.

------◆◆◆------

21

COMPOSTING

YES, YES, COMPOSTING DISPOSES of organic waste — watermelon rinds, peanut shells, avocado skins — but as every gardener knows, the real benefit is what you harvest: fertilizer; mulch; with some mineral additions, good soil. Use a thermometer and a recipe, keep it wet, keep it turned, and cut stuff small. Red wigglers can help. Animal manure, if you have it, is an excellent source of nitrogen. Nurture your trash, and it'll nurture you.

Research shows that simply by increasing organic matter in their fields from 1 to 5 percent, farmers can increase water storage in plants' root zones from 33 pounds per cubic meter to 195 pounds.

◆ ◆

22

CONVERSING

THE GRACEFUL ART OF GIVE AND TAKE, back and forth, banter and repartee, congratulations and condolences, digressions and exaggerations is one of the most pleasurable activities we humans indulge in. Conversation requires less manual dexterity than typing, less between-the-lines interpretation than reading a letter or e-mail, and far less pithiness than a tweet. Conversation can twist or veer depending on company or privacy, body language or atmosphere, beverage or music. Good conversation nurtures as surely as good food.

◆ ◆ ◆

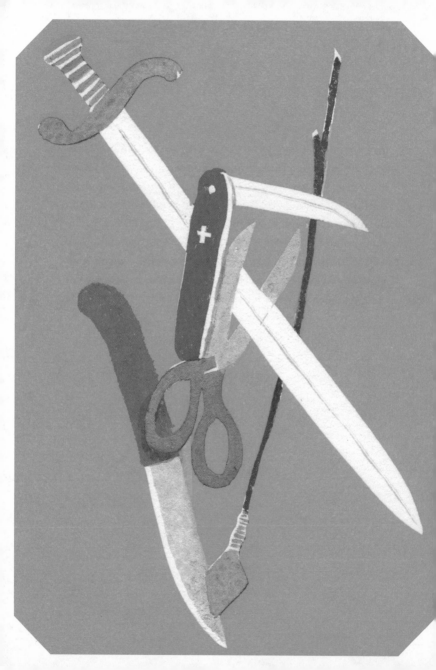

23

CUTLERING

TO CUT FOOD OR BUILD SHELTER, to clean a wound or butcher an animal, no tool is more valuable than a knife. Cutlering is the art of making edged cutting tools: knives, razors, scissors, swords, and spears. The simplest knives are knapped stone, basalt or obsidian, wedged in split green wood and tied in place with bark or sinew or stems. A blacksmith can forge a sword in fire. Any aspiring cutler can practice with a metal-cutting band saw, a grinder, and a scribe. Fashion handles from ivory, antlers, or wood. Don't forget a sheath.

24

DAYDREAMING

WHY IS IT WE CAN RESEARCH or brainstorm or concentrate all we want and still the best ideas pop into our heads while standing in the shower or walking to work or lying on the beach or staring at the wall? That's when the imagination kicks in. That's where inventions originate. Telling yourself to be creative works about as well as telling yourself to be funny — not very well. So plan some downtime, find some quiet space, and dream away.

Daydreaming works in the middle of the night, too, if you can sacrifice some shut-eye. (See also: *Sleeping.*)

25

DENTAL HEALTH

LET'S OMIT THE STRING-AND-DOORKNOB FOR NOW. Ditto for the pliers. Before we start thinking about pulling a permanent tooth, as opposed to a baby tooth destined for the Tooth Fairy, let's consider prevention and early detection. The same ho-hum advice we learned, and sometimes ignored, in grade school will apply in the future.

Avoid too much sugar. Brush morning and night. Floss daily. If you can't find the store-bought variety or prefer a nonplastic alternative, try silk thread or agave leaves. For an alternative mouthwash try coconut oil, or water with a few drops of antiseptic tea tree or lavender oil.

If a problem arises, there are home remedies to try. If you get a toothache, rinse with salt water or try a dab of clove oil. Sucking ice cubes can help in certain situations. For painful gums, try ginseng. For a lost filling, try a wad of wax. If worse comes to worst, you will need forceps, a good anesthetic, gauze packing, and hopefully good directions to find someone with training.

26

DISPOSING OF TRASH

NO MATTER HOW HARD YOU TRY TO CONSUME LITTLE, to reuse what you have, to plant and forage and build sustainably, you will create trash. Burn it or bury it, separate it and clean it. But do so carefully. It's easy enough to find a place for, say, bones or bricks or iron. Bones will decompose; used bricks have a thousand uses; leached iron is nontoxic. But what about painted plywood, used batteries, carpet scraps, caulk?

Too many materials we humans strove to invent or extract, from plastic to Freon to cadmium, can wreak havoc. And they aren't going anywhere soon. So be aware: when you burn, you may create dangerous fumes; when you bury, you may contaminate water sources; when you separate hazardous waste, you may risk exposure.

Make a plan thoughtfully, communicate it clearly, and monitor it regularly. (See also: *Revising.*)

◆ ◆ ◆

27
DOWSING

MAYBE YOU'VE READ STORIES and not quite believed. Try it anyway. Cut a longish whip of one-year-old deciduous wood (apple or dogwood, willow or hazel, birch or beech; many species work well) with a forked end. Grasp either end of the fork loosely in your hands and walk slowly until the straight end quivers and bends. Sometimes the twig will bend gingerly, other times dramatically. The stronger the bend, the more water you'll find.

If that doesn't work, cut two pieces of heavy-gauge wire. Coat hangers work in a pinch. Bend them into Ls. Hold them loosely, with the long end of each L outstretched, and walk until they quiver and diverge. The straight line they tend toward will parallel an underground watercourse.

If that doesn't work either, don't worry. Dowsing seems to have little to do with practice or faith. (Maybe that's why some people call it "witching.") Find someone who has the gift. Be ready to dig!

◆ ◆ ◆

28

DRY FARMING

EVEN IF YOU LIVE IN A SEMI-ARID REGION, if you consider the difficulty of hauling or collecting water long enough, you start to contemplate growing food without irrigation. So-called "dry farming" does just that through a combination of drought-resistant crops, careful cultivation, and heavy mulch. In places like the Mediterranean and California, the practice has a long tradition.

The downside is that you need more space than you might for irrigated crops. The upside is that you can raise a remarkable variety of produce: tomatoes, pumpkins, watermelons, cantaloupes, winter squash, olives, garbanzos, apricots, apples, and potatoes. What's more, the fruits and vegetables tend to taste better, since less water content means a greater density of sugars, and they tend to store better, too, since they're less susceptible to rot.

One caveat: You'll need a minimum of rain, 15 to 20 inches a year, to build up the groundwater table. Las Vegas is out of luck; Lubbock stands a chance.

29

FALCONRY

NOT MUCH OF A HUNTER? You can train raptors to hunt wild quarry — birds and small mammals — for you. For centuries, the ancient art of falconry was a pastime of European royalty, a way to gain status, and UNESCO recognized its value by adding it to The List of Intangible Cultural Heritage of Humanity. But this one-time "sport" can have tangible benefits, too. Trained birds of prey can, for instance, rid orchards and vineyards of gophers, squirrels, and mice.

In most states, hunting with raptors is as legal as hunting with a gun or a bow or dogs. The time commitment is more serious, though: a long-term apprenticeship with a mentor is the norm.

At some point, with help from your mentor, you'll capture a young falcon or hawk and begin to forge a bond that may last years. You'll keep the raptor in an enclosure called a *mews* and take it out to hunt each day. Many falconers today fit their raptors with telemetry in case they fly off. In a changed world, you may have to rely on trust.

◆ ◆ ◆

30
FENCE BUILDING

"GOOD FENCES MAKE GOOD NEIGHBORS," claims the proverb. But they do so much more. Fences protect children and animals, privacy and property, grave sites and water sources and food. Any gardener can tell you: it's one thing to plant a garden, and quite another to nurture the plants through harvest. Too many other creatures are eager to share the bounty.

Build the fence first, and save yourself the heartache. Use what you have: chicken wire or concrete mesh, cedar or cacti or rocks. Build a wattle with twigs or branches or reeds. A solar panel can power electric wires for as long as the batteries hold out. Make it tall and make it strong and make it smart.

Think like a rabbit: where might you burrow? Think like a deer: where might you leap? Think like the enemy when you design your gates. Who will watch them? How will they latch? Who might try to enter, and how will you keep them out?

Fair warning: If you don't build it, they will come.

31

FINANCIAL LITERACY

BASIC INVENTORY AND BOOKKEEPING aren't nearly as fun as, say, blacksmithing or weaving, but they may be more necessary in a more localized, less global economy. Whether for personal use or in a small handmade business, money management is critical. It's great to barter when you can, to practice frugality as much as possible, but at some point financial interactions, like all human interactions, get tricky.

Learn to use a spreadsheet without a computer. Relearn arithmetic without a calculator. Keep records. Pay bills on time. Think budget and cash flow, debt management and cost overruns. The more you understand, the better off you'll be.

◆◆◆

32

FINDING YOUR WAY

ON WATER. If the Polynesians could crisscross the Pacific navigating by the stars, we can, too. Read Thor Heyerdahl's *Kon-Tiki* for inspiration and a good star chart for elucidation. Remember: before planes, trains, and automobiles, travel by water was faster and easier than by land.

Which suggests a sea kayak purchase might be in order. Or an outrigger canoe.

ON LAND. You can check for moss on the north side of trees, but where it's wet, moss will grow on all sides. You can depend on the stars, but in cloudy weather or deep woods or a steep valley, that gets iffy. Your best bets are a map and compass.

Maps are endlessly useful. Study the legend, note the intervals between contour lines, match the squirreling topographic lines to features on the land, whether mountains or mesas, canyons or creeks. A compass is lightweight and reliable as long as you adjust for declination (the difference between magnetic and true north). An altimeter doesn't hurt if you're in the mountains.

Then there's this: when you are lost, stop and ask directions. Better than GPS any day.

FINDING YOUR WAY BY SUN

Use an analog watch to find approximate north and south.

NORTHERN HEMISPHERE: Holding the watch flat, point the hour hand in the sun's direction. South is halfway between the hour hand and 12:00 (or 1:00 during daylight saving time, spring to fall).

SOUTHERN HEMISPHERE: Point the numeral 12 at the sun. North is halfway between the hour hand and the 12.

NORTH/
SOUTH AXIS

FINDING YOUR WAY BY STARS & MOON

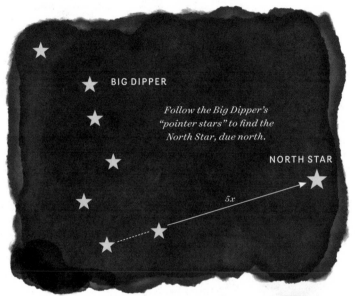

BIG DIPPER

Follow the Big Dipper's "pointer stars" to find the North Star, due north.

NORTH STAR

5x

A first-quarter moon rises in the east at about noon and sets in the west at about midnight. Its bright side points toward the west, because it is trailing the sun.

A last-quarter moon rises in the east at about midnight and sets in the west at about noon. Its bright side will point toward the east, because it is leading the sun.

west

FIRST-QUARTER MOON

east

LAST-QUARTER MOON

33

FIRE FIGHTING

SMOKEY THE BEAR IS RIGHT: Only we can prevent forest fires. We can put out our campfires cold, watch the size of our brush piles, and keep matches away from children. But we can't prevent them all. While scientists agree that we need to let some burn, we also know that we must protect our homes and crops and neighbors.

A major blaze may demand a tanker truck or retardant plane, but if the fire is still manageable, there's a lot you can do by hand. You can get a long way with a shovel and a bladder bag — a backpack of water, like an oversized CamelBak with a nozzle. Use the shovel to dig down to mineral soil to build a containment line around the fire. Use the bladder bag to spray water on coals to keep a smoldering fire from reigniting.

When you're done, drag the back of your hand across the coals — "cold trailing," it's called — to make sure your fire is out cold. Just like Smokey says.

◆◆◆

34

FIRE MAKING

USE FLINT AND STEEL, or quartzite and a pocket knife, to make a spark. Use glass to direct sunlight onto dry tinder. If you don't have glass, try a balloon filled with water or a thin, polished piece of ice or the concave bottom of a clear plastic bottle.

Or try the bow drill: take a dry straight stick — a spindle — and a cedar board, milled or split. Carve a triangle wedge in the board big enough to hold the stick. Set the stick in it and spin it between your palms. Spin until you have a small pile of embers to set in a tangle of tinder: dry grass or cedar shavings, a wasp nest, wax or moss or pine pitch.

After tinder, you'll need kindling: dry twigs or straight sticks or strips of bark. Finally comes fuel: not green, not wet, not poison oak, god forbid. Leave enough room for air.

Once you have the flame, keep it alive.

35

FLETCHING

THAT'S MAKING BOWS AND ARROWS to you and me. Fletching is all about stabilization: you add three feathers at the base of an arrow, relative to the length of the shaft, like the three fins at the base of a rocket ship. Same principle, different scale. You can use feathers from almost any species of bird; a wing feather is best.

For a bow, you'll need a green limb or stave split from a green tree or straight-grained board at least 6 feet long. Maple, willow, yew, oak, or hickory will do. Cut a notch — called a "nock" — in either end and secure the bowstring (sinew, silk, rawhide, linen, hemp) with a sturdy knot, and if you've got it, a drop of glue. Experiment with length for power.

Practice, practice, practice. Set up a target and a backdrop (hay or soft wood or an old mattress) about 10 yards away. Mark the area clearly. Check your equipment and your clothing (no loose sleeves!), and fire away. Making bows and arrows, like shooting them, is easy enough to do poorly but takes experience to do well.

◆ ◆ ◆

36
FORAGING LOCALLY

THERE'S KELP ALONG THE COAST, super-rich in folic acid and vitamin K; prickly pear in the desert (remove the spines first!); and miner's lettuce in the woods: good raw, steamed, fried, or pickled.

On the calorie-maximization scale, berry picking is not the most efficient activity, but on the delight scale, it's off the charts. Strawberries in spring. Raspberries in cream. *Blueberries for Sal.* Huckleberries in the mountains in pancakes sticky with juice. Thimbleberries in an alley.

You can even forage in the city. Join a group in Los Angeles, New York, Chicago, or San Francisco, and you'll learn where to harvest native plants, find garden also-rans like Jerusalem artichokes or feral rhubarb or asparagus, or glean from abandoned fruit and nut trees and grapevines. You'll learn, too, to avoid auto repair shops and factories where plants can be contaminated from emissions.

Wherever you forage, be prepared. Carry gloves, a gallon-sized ziplock, or a small spade. And be careful. Wild onion, for example, looks a lot like death camas.

◆ ◆

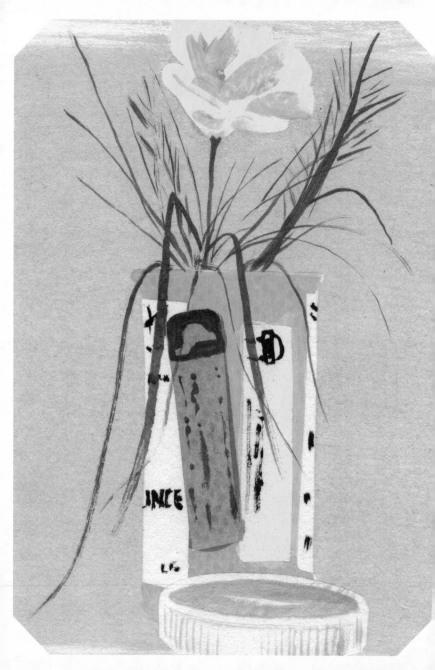

37

FORAGING MEDICINALS

ETHNOBOTANISTS HAVE DONE HALF THE WORK for us, cataloging the knowledge of indigenous people — from the Chinese to the Mayans to the Australian Aborigines and North American Indians — who've healed themselves with the plants that surround them for millennia. Today, by some estimates, as much as 80 percent of the world's population depends on medicine derived directly from plants.

The specifics differ by region, but the list is long. This will get you started.

Forage ginger for the stomach, wild yam for morning sickness, California poppies for anxiety, mint for a headache, catnip for a cold, aloe vera for sunburn. Substitute sage for ibuprofen, blackberry root for Campho-Phenique (to heal mouth sores), ferns for Bactine (to ease minor stings, cuts, and burns).

It's one thing to collect the right plants — wildcrafting — and another to know how to prepare them, as tinctures or teas, for ingestion or application or inhalation. The knowledge exists; it's a matter of chasing it down.

MEDICINAL HERBS

GOLDENSEAL
*fights infections, colds,
and flus*

PLANTAIN
*draws out slivers;
helps check bleeding*

ELDER
*stimulates immune system;
lowers fever*

CHAMOMILE
*treats arthritis and other
inflammations*

HAWTHORN
*strengthens the heart;
regulates blood pressure*

RED CLOVER
*relieves symptoms of
menopause*

MULLEIN
*aids respiratory
stress*

DANDELION
*cleanses and stimulates the liver;
aids digestion*

38

FORAGING WEEDS

DANDELIONS ARE THE PRIZEWINNERS. You can collect young leaves (before they blossom) for salads or use the taproot in soup, fry the flowers into fritters or ferment them into wine. Dandelions have more beta-carotene than carrots, more iron than spinach.

But they're not alone. Edible weeds include other garden creepers like purslane (garnish a salad or pickle the stems) and stinging nettles (wear gloves, and serve cooked, never raw), field dwellers like cattails (the lowest part of the stem tastes like corn), and even damaging invasives like Japanese knotweed (use the tangy new shoots in spring as you might use rhubarb). Don't forget lamb's-quarter, sorrel, plantain, mustard, even (lucky you!) clover.

The list is long, the food is free, and weeding can become a lot more fun.

◆ ◆ ◆

39

FRUGALITY

IF DEBT CAN BE A PRISON, frugality can mean freedom. When you owe nothing, you can live independently. Frugality means pinching pennies, of course, but also using all parts of a thing — deer antlers as knife handles, cedar bark as siding; even the foliage of a sweet potato is edible. More than anything, frugality means keeping track of what you have and what you need, balancing the two, and avoiding waste. If "growth for growth's sake is the philosophy of the cancer cell," as Edward Abbey famously wrote, then scaling back, choosing to make do with less, might be the key to sustainability. Or even survival.

40

GLEANING

THE TRADITION IS LONG. Gleaning — collecting what's left over in a field after harvest — is addressed in Old Testament teachings and portrayed in Van Gogh paintings; it was officially sanctioned by the French in the Middle Ages and by the Oregon legislature in the 1970s. In its modern incarnation, the practice happens everywhere, from Freegans dumpster-diving for pizzas in New York City to gypsies gathering fallen apples in Greece, from garage-salers resurrecting hand tools and dusty first editions on suburban Saturday mornings to volunteers picking up day-old baked goods at Starbucks for a food bank.

Suppose the future world splinters into haves and have-nots: gleaning will prove useful whichever side you fall on. If you're in need, find what's left and use it. If you're doing all right, find what's left and share it.

◆ ◆ ◆

41
GLIDING

FLIGHT WITHOUT FUEL IS EASY . . . if you're courageous. You can pack a paraglider to the top of a mountain and leap. The wing can span a mere 200 square feet; the whole rig can weigh less than 50 pounds. You're a human kite!

For greater range and a tad more security, try a hang glider. Record breakers have reached over 35,000 feet in altitude and traveled over 400 miles. A fixed-wing glider takes many forms, though it still requires outside power for takeoff or extended flights or in case of engine failure.

Whatever mode you choose, you'll have to learn to read the wind. Thermals will lift you from the sun-heated earth. Ridge lift takes charge when you launch from a hill. You'll have to learn basic flight dynamics, too: the roll (side to side), the yaw (front to back vertical), and the pitch (front to back horizontal).

Of course, not everyone is destined to fly. Not to worry. The thrill of gliding is still within reach: skate, ski, ride a bicycle with no hands, try ballroom dancing. Glide away.

◆ ◆ ◆

42

GRAFFITI

PAINT THE WALLS, CARVE THE ROCKS, write it big in symbols or pictures. For signage or bookkeeping or worship, for staking a claim or expressing rage or illustrating a story, graffiti is the most durable art form we've got.

Someone's distant ancestors painted caves in Spain, France, and Australia 40,000 years ago, and their messages remain. The Anasazi in Utah etched handprints, spirals, animals, and alien-seeming creatures into sandstone 800 years ago, then disappeared. Kids use spray paint on railroad overpasses. Big-time artists use fiberglass and canvas and cast iron downtown. Graffiti is a way to preserve alphabets, honor the dead, make your mark.

Or you can use it to make a joke. Deep in one high alpine forest stands an aspen tree into which these immortal words are meticulously carved in backwards script: *Help! I can't get out!*

❖ ❖ ❖

43

GRAFTING

FOR EARLY SETTLERS, nothing symbolized self-sufficiency more than growing your own fruit — better than a bunker of canned goods any day. But plant an apple seed and you get sour apples. A seed-grown tree produces crabapples: good for cider, maybe, but lousy for eating.

To get sizable, recognizable fruit, you graft. You cut a whip of new growth — your "scion" — usually the diameter of a pencil, from a tasty variety. With a small sharp knife, you slice the bark of your crabapple tree — now considered your "rootstock" — and you slip the scion wood in, paying careful attention to ensure cambium matches cambium. You wrap the wound with grafting tape, paint it with grafting paint, and wait a few weeks to see if new growth appears. If it does, your graft has taken.

Heritage apple guru Tom Burford encourages everyone who knows how to graft to teach five others. If you know how, start now. Bring Band-Aids.

44

GROWING RURAL

SAY YOU HAVE A LOT OF FERTILE ACREAGE, and you already have a garden chock-full of enough favorite vegetables to share with neighbors: what's the best crop to grow to provide for the future?

There'd be a lot of votes for corn; so much sugar means so many calories. Then again, peas and beans provide protein and fix nitrogen in the soil. Someone might suggest amaranth — easy to grow almost anywhere — but if you've ever tried to winnow a season's worth, well, you understand the problem. Okra or squash? Pumpkins or cabbage? Potatoes are excellent, but look what monoculture did to Ireland. Any crop can, of course, become a monoculture.

So we're back to the first rule of sustainable agriculture: plant a variety. Don't forget to cover-crop in the off-season. Alfalfa or vetch or winter wheat or buckwheat? Decisions, decisions.

◆ ◆ ◆

45

GROWING URBAN

EVEN IN A VERY SMALL YARD, you can plant raised beds. (Salvage the lumber, conserve and nourish the soil, aerate regularly, rotate your crops.) No yard at all? You can plant the rooftop. (Watch the weight load, drain the water, harness the rain, maximize sunlight.) Got a front yard? Yank the lawn and plant veggies. The neighbors will complain only until harvest season.

Plant anywhere and everywhere. Guerrilla gardeners know how it's done: find a vacant lot or a median. Find cheap plants or free ones. Transplant starts from culverts or roadsides where they'll otherwise be removed. Choose hardy varieties and watch for noxious weeds, grumpy landowners, and city officials.

◆ ◆ ◆

46

HANDWRITING

HANDWRITING HAS BEEN IN SERIOUS DECLINE since at least the Apple II era. Even nuns don't teach cursive anymore. But how will we communicate if we don't have LED screens? Smoke signals? Passenger pigeons? Probably not.

Paper makes up 40 percent of all municipal waste; we should have enough to last awhile before we fall back on sheepskin. And no need for disposable ballpoints. You can write with a fountain pen or a quill — a primary wing-feather, most likely from a goose. The ancient Romans used a hollow reed. (See also: *Ink Making*.) Pencils are easy to make if you have access to the so-called lead, a mix of graphite and clay. If not, you can write with chalk or, in a bind, with charcoal.

Hand-write a love letter or a thank-you card. Leave the babysitter a note. Send the boss a memo. The essential ingredient: legibility.

———◆◆◆———

47
HIDING

YOU CAN MOVE STEALTHILY AMONG PREDATORS or build a fort in a tree, stay under the covers or change your name. You can hide in the woods, unafraid of solitude, or tuck shoulder-to-shoulder into a vast concert crowd, unafraid of anonymity. You can hide from enemies, like Bin Laden did in Pakistan or Eichmann did in Argentina or Butch Cassidy did in the Outlaw Cave, or you can hide with friends like the 200 elementary school kids in Rockdale, Georgia, who played hide-and-seek all at once to try to break the world record.

Both fight and flight have their downsides. Hide instead. For safety and for fun.

◆ ◆ ◆

48

HOARDING

WHAT SECRET KNOWLEDGE do your Depression-era grand-parents share with the homeless woman pushing her shopping cart and the neighbor guy futzing in a garage that will never, ever have space enough for a motorbike, much less a car? They know that stuff is useful, and waste is wasteful, and you never know what you'll need next.

Anyone who's gone without or feared going without knows the drill: don't toss it out! Hang on to scraps and screws, hardware and hoses, paper for kindling and communication, metal for welding, boards for building or burning. Store it where you can. On the porch or in the drawer, on your back or in the forest duff or behind a cinderblock wall in the abandoned Kmart parking lot.

Even though hoarding gets a bad rap nowadays when there's a Home Depot on every corner, in the future *not* reducing might be the key to recycling and reusing.

◆ ◆

49

HOME BREWING

THOSE OLD OLYMPIA BEER COMMERCIALS had it right: *It's in the water.* Anyone can make a decent ale with clean, clear, chlorine-free water. You'll need a pot, some grains, some yeast, and hops. Hops grow like weeds; you can harvest the flowers and dry them or use them fresh. Boil the grains, add the hops, cool the liquid — now called the "wort" — and add yeast. Then wait a week or three. Keeping everything clean is crucial (as it is in butchering and childbirth). Practicing with flavors is fun.

Start now. Shipping all that water weight around the country is senseless, as is disposing of all those cans and bottles. The world to come might be one of deprivation — who knows? — but at least we will have good ale. Pilsner and lager come later.

◆ ◆

50

HOME CHILDBIRTH

FEW CONVERSATIONS ARE AS POLARIZED as those surrounding home birth. Some women worry that there are too many caesarean sections — about a third of all births in the United States today — and too many hospital births induced (or worse, planned), to accommodate doctors' schedules. As a result they choose to have babies at home, with time and space to give birth more naturally. Others, including some medical professionals, claim that this choice is unsafe, even selfish.

The debate rages. But what if our dependency on expensive equipment and facilities makes hospital births unrealistic, at least for some mothers? The solution is expertise, and there's no shortage. A midwife — a trained professional who can deal, for example, with a breech birth or twins — practices in a time-honored tradition. A doula or labor coach can support mother and family before, during, and after the birth.

If we can figure out how to forge tools from iron and fire or to navigate by the stars, surely we can learn how best to bear children at home.

51

HORSE & MULE HANDLING

HORSES AND MULES CAN TAKE YOU LONG DISTANCES — much farther than walking — and pull wagons, sleds, and plows. They can haul logs out of the woods and hay off the fields and camping gear over the steepest mountain passes. Mules eat less, live longer, and are more sure-footed than horses. Horses are better leaders, faster runners, and taller animals, so a rider can see over a herd or a field or a pack string.

Both are large animals, apt to kick, bite, trample, or buck when trying to escape perceived danger. To protect yourself, be calm and confident. Pet the shoulder and neck, not the nose, and avoid standing directly behind the animal. Watch for a swishing tail or flattened ears, signs of agitation. You may have to learn to use a hobble, a twitch, a muzzle, or a blindfold.

But mostly, you will care for them: feed and water and groom them, pick out their hooves, breed them and foal them. You'll nurse them when they're sick and keep their stables clean, day after day, week after week, year after year, shoveling out precious manure that you can compost for your garden.

EQUINE BODY LANGUAGE

What the Ears Are Saying

alert and friendly

afraid

angry

attentive

unhappy or sick

bored or tired

What the Tail Is Saying

excited

submissive

alarmed or playful

HARNESSING HORSES AND MULES

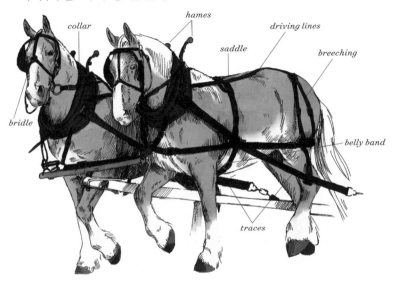

collar · _hames_ · _driving lines_ · _saddle_ · _breeching_ · _bridle_ · _belly band_ · _traces_

Steps in Harnesssing

1. COLLAR

2. HAMES

3. SADDLE, TRACES, AND BREECHING

4. LOWER STRAPS AND BELLY BAND

5. BRIDLE

6. DRIVING LINES

Parts of the Bridle

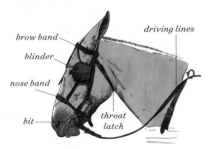

brow band · _driving lines_ · _blinder_ · _nose band_ · _bit_ · _throat latch_

52

HOUSEGUEST HOSTING

NO MORE THREE-DAYS-AND-THEY-STINK PRIVILEGES. Ask people who travel by foot or in the developing world, and they'll tell you: if it takes a long time to travel somewhere, you're going to stay awhile. Ask the underemployed — more every day — and they'll tell you: a friend's couch beats a hotel any day. So we need to be prepared.

Keep clean sheets on hand. Save up on food. And patience. Put your houseguests to work — splitting firewood, shucking corn, hauling supplies, washing dishes or above-mentioned sheets — to lighten your load and to make your guests feel at home. Swap stories or play music to make the visit fun.

53
HUNTING

SOME PEOPLE BELIEVE HUNTING IS A CRITICAL SKILL, one that dictated our need for tools that in turn enlarged our brains. Others believe it's inhumane. Some claim we need to control invasive species and to keep game populations in check in the absence of natural predators. Others say starvation, disease, and low fertility will take care of that. Some claim hunting provides clean, low-cost meat; others say it's cheaper to raise your own.

If you want to try, where should you begin?

Find a mentor. Learn about the area where you intend to hunt and the tool you intend to use: a gun or a bow, a spear for fishing. Practice often so you won't miss and injure an animal. Learn about your animal, track its movements. Make yourself invisible and eliminate your own smell. Consider the wind. Wait and wait and wait. Do not move at all.

When it is time to kill, be steady and sure. If the animal moves after you've shot, you'll need to track it, no matter how long it takes. Gut the animal and pack it out, keeping the meat as cool as possible. (See also: *Butchering.*)

ANIMAL TRACKS

COYOTE

RED FOX

DOMESTIC CAT

SKUNK

GRAY SQUIRREL

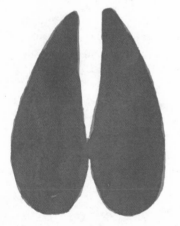

MOOSE

ELK

OPOSSUM

RACCOON

MUSKRAT

GROUNDHOG

WHITETAIL DEER

COTTONTAIL RABBIT

WILD TURKEY

125

10
30
70
50

72
69
66
60
5.7

NYPD
2 34 99 147
MOREL

54

IDENTIFYING MUSHROOMS

EDIBLE WILD MUSHROOMS are plentiful and nutritious: rich in protein, calcium, and potassium, and the only vegetable source of vitamin D. Some mushrooms are, of course, poisonous. Intense stomach pain leading to kidney or liver damage or even death can result from ingesting even a grain of the wrong species. So certain identification is crucial.

Pictures aren't your best bet. Instead start with the morphological features. (A good field guide will lay them out: the shape and structure of the stalk and cap, for example, or the method by which the gills attach.) Then move on to color. If necessary, use a magnifying glass. A knowledgeable neighbor will help, as will sticking to common varieties: chanterelles, morels, oyster mushrooms, puffballs.

Watch the weather. A dry spell after some rain can bode a bumper crop, as can a wet spring after a fall forest fire. Wind can affect dispersal, so don't count on one good spot to last.

Harvest in moderation, and avoid taking morels, especially, when they're small. (A rule of thumb: Never pick morels smaller than your thumb.)

55

INK MAKING

NEARLY ALL THE INK WE USE these days is petroleum-based. Who knew? There was a move toward soy and vegetable-based inks during the 1970s oil crisis, and you can still find them in environmentally friendly printer ink, but there are other options. For centuries humans made ink with carbon, berry juice, tree bark, or animal skins. We can do it again.

The ingredients are everywhere. Vinegar and salt. Tannic acid squeezed from teabags or found in peaty streams. Egg yolks and honey. Galls (growths on the stems of plants), ground to a powder. Lamp black from a dripping candle.

Find a recipe, wear old clothes, and make your mark. (See also: *Handwriting.*)

———◆◆◆———

56
KNITTING

WHAT CONJURES UP WARMTH AND PRODUCTIVITY more than knitting? With needles and yarn and some time on your hands, you can knit hats or sweaters or socks by the dozen. Knitting makes travel faster, long winter nights shorter, and the knitter — male especially — more attractive to mates.

Learn the basics: the knit stitch and the purl. Use these to create the stockinette, garter, and seed stitches. Watch out always for the dropped stitch. Mix colors and textures, and add popcorn, cables, or pom-poms for fun. Knit wool or silk, angora or twine. Research shows we listen better when our hands are busy, and that paying close attention reduces stress and the chance of dementia.

Warning: Needles can be mistaken for weapons, so keep the yarn close.

◆◆◆

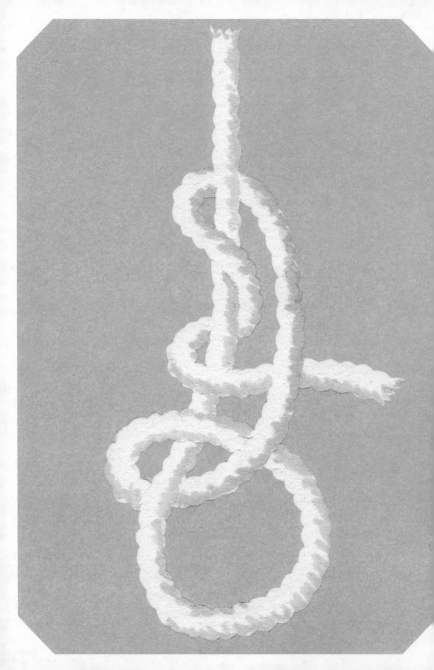

57
KNOT TYING

FIND A SHOELACE and a copy of *The Ashley Book of Knots.*
Knots can make rugs, string snowshoes, or raise sails. A
diamond hitch holds a load on a mule or a sled. A water knot
connects one short scrap to another. Use a bowline to cinch
a tarp, a Prusik to climb a tree, a weaver's knot to build a
cane chair. You *must* know knots to summit Mt. Everest,
to perform surgery, to fly-fish, or to tat a doily. You *can* use
knots to fashion a ladder or lasso a calf or rescue a fall vic-
tim from a tight spot.

And knots can repair almost anything. Need to fix a splin-
tered shovel handle? Try parachute cord and pine pitch.
A fishing net with holes? A simple sheet bend or a double
hitch will do.

(See also: *Snowshoe Crafting, Sailing, Splicing, Rigging,
Horse & Mule Handling.* The list could go on and on.)

KNOTS EVERYONE
SHOULD KNOW

Parts of the Rope

1. THE STANDING PART
*The long, unused portion
of the rope on which you
work*

2. THE BIGHT
*The loop formed whenever
the rope is turned back
upon itself*

3. THE TAIL
*The short end you use in
tying*

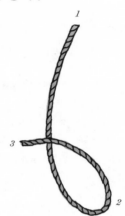

Basic Knots

OVERHAND KNOT
*Start with the
position shown
in the diagram
here. Turn the tail
through the bight
from back to front
and draw tight.*

**FIGURE-EIGHT
KNOT**
*Start as before. Lead
the tail around the
standing part and
through the bight
from front to back.*

Knots for Tying Ropes Together

SQUARE OR REEF KNOT
This knot never slips or jams and is easy to tie and untie. Good choice for first-aid bandaging.

SHEET BEND OR WEAVER'S KNOT
Make a bight with one rope and then pass the tail of the other rope up through and around the entire bight, bending it under its own standing part.

tail

THE BOWLINE
Form a small loop on the standing part. Pass the tail up through the bight around the standing part and down through the bight again. To tighten, hold noose in position and pull standing part.

TWO HALF HITCHES
These knots will not slip under any strain. Diagram shows simple tying technique.

CLOVE HITCH
Used to fasten a rope to a pole, this knot holds snugly and will not slip laterally. Hold the standing part in left hand, then pass the tail around the pole. Cross the standing part, making a second turn around the pole, and pass the tail under the last turn.

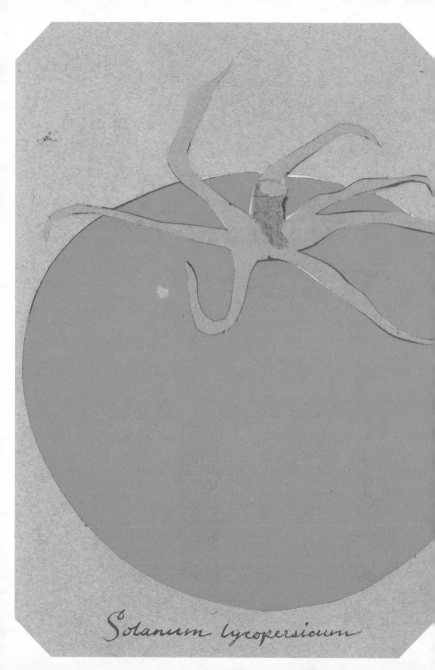

Solanum lycopersicum

58

LATIN NAMES

WHETHER YOU PLAN TO HARVEST mushrooms for dinner or logs for a bridge, to raise chickens or collect wildflower seeds or attract ladybugs, knowing the differences among species is critical. The problem with common names is that they change from region to region, sometimes from household to household. Is that a red fir or a Doug fir? A silver fir or a piss fir? Hen of the woods or maitake? Cowslip or shooting star?

Scientists figured out the solution centuries ago: one language. Latin. Every species on earth gets a two-part name: genus first, species second. Many are descriptive, suggesting characteristics (long ears, say, or hard seeds); others reflect common names used by indigenous people, and plenty are named for famous people: scientists and monarchs, rock stars and comedians.

Any good guidebook can teach you the names. It's up to you, out in the field, to make the connections . . . and the distinctions. (See also: *Memorizing*.)

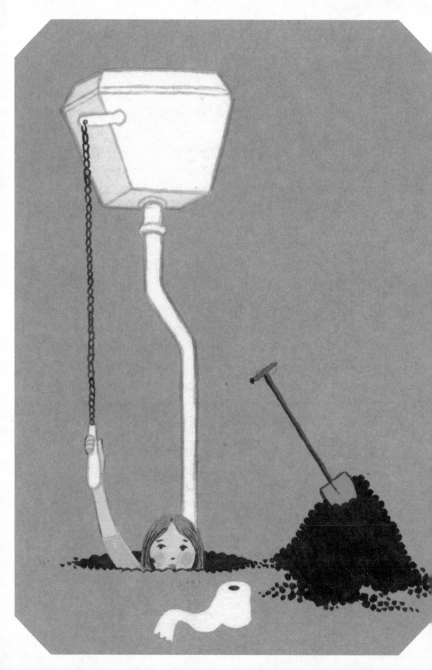

59

LATRINE DIGGING

FIND A WELL-DRAINED SPOT, downhill from any water source, above the water table and out of the floodplain. For long-term use by a family or a small group, dig a hole roughly as deep as you are tall. (Warning: No deeper or you'll have to shore up the sides; people have died digging outhouse holes.) The World Health Organization recommends a hole capacity of 0.06 cubic meter (2.12 cubic feet) per person per year. You can start with a shovel and rock bar, but eventually you'll lie on your belly and pull up handfuls of dirt, an excellent if awkward core workout.

Install a seat or a squat hole with footrests. Add ash or lime to keep down the smell, and sawdust to keep the oxygen level high so aerobic bacteria can do their thing. Keep the lid closed to keep out flies. Check for spiders before you sit. Set up a hand-washing station for after. When the hole fills up, cover thoroughly and dig anew.

60
LAUGHING

LAUGHTER IS CONTAGIOUS — just hearing someone laugh makes us laugh more — and laughter is instinctual. We laugh when our expectations are thwarted by clever irony (*The Onion* or *The Colbert Report*) or by plain surprise (a pie in the face, a banana peel slip). Laughter is healthy: it relaxes our muscles and distracts us from pain, and like sex and meditation and exercise, it releases endorphins, increases blood flow, and boosts immunity.

Humor helps us make friends, create allies, and attract mates. A shared chuckle cuts through tension like a knife through soft butter. But really, why do we need laughter? Because without it, life in any age would be too cruel to comprehend.

———◆◆◆———

61

LISTENING

YOU CAN LISTEN FOR AN ELK BUGLE or an approaching storm, to a symphony or a baby crying in an adjacent room or the rattling breath of someone on the edge of death. You can listen to a bad joke or a too-long story, to someone who's been wronged and needs to say so, over and over. You can listen to a child tell a tale about dragons that spirals out and never resolves.

No one has ever suffered from having been listened to too well. Teachers or preachers or counselors or parents might weary of listening, but no one regrets it in the end. Listening allows us to clear up misunderstandings, consider other perspectives, practice empathy, and learn new skills. Without listeners, storytellers and musicians alike are useless.

———◆◆◆———

62

MEMORIZING

MEMORIZE A YEATS POEM or a Bible verse. Memorize the digits of pi out to the 31st decimal and match the record of three-year-old Grace Hare. (No kidding.) Memorize directions to the nearest swimming hole or the best berry patch. Memorize azimuths and addresses. Memorize soliloquies from Shakespeare, passages of lost novels or phrases in lost languages.

Memorization frees up time you'd spend looking up information and space you'd use storing or carrying maps and reference books. Memorization is good for the brain: it strengthens the synapses, benefits the hippocampus, and teaches rhythmic patterns. Some experts believe it can stave off cognitive decline.

There's social value, too. If you find yourself spending time with someone who needs a little spiritual uplift or comic relief or elucidation, scroll through the memory queue. There's probably something there. (See also: *Storytelling*.)

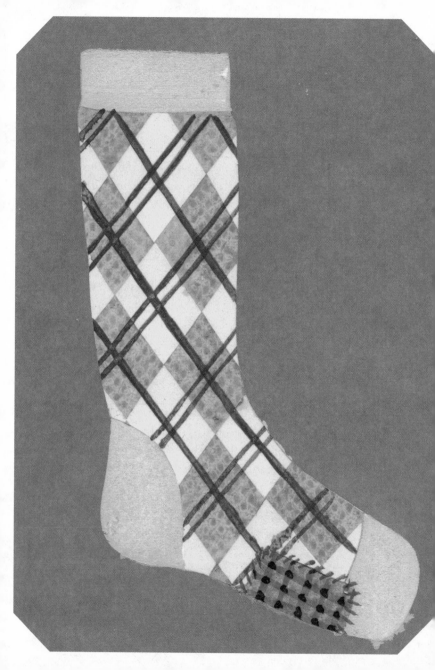

63

MENDING

DEF. 1. Repairing something broken, torn, worn, or unusable

To get the most out of your clothing: mend. Restitch seams, replace buttons, and reinforce knees. Catch tears early before they run. Use good thread always and colorful thread if you'd like.

To mend holes in socks or sweaters: darn. You'll need a darning egg (a ball of wood or stone to hold the hole in place) and a strong, dull needle with a large eye to accommodate yarn. (See also: *Patching.*)

DEF. 2. Mending fences; reconciling or forgiving

Friendships, alliances, and tenuous truces can all be damaged. It takes so little: a misspoken word or a petty disagreement, an outright dispute or a spell of stagnation. It might be hard to take that first step, to give in a little, to forgive, to start anew, but everyone knows: relationships are more important, even, than socks or sweaters. Mend them early. Make them last.

———————◆—◆———————

64

MUSIC MAKING

MUSIC IS INSPIRING, timeless, and universal. Every culture in the world plays music, composes music, listens to music. Music passes the time — screen-free entertainment — and it's portable, besides. You probably can't travel with a piano, but a banjo, guitar, trumpet, or fiddle can fit in a pack. A harmonica fits in a pocket. Then there are makeshift instruments, like the washboard, but who has a washboard even at the end of the world as we know it? Try spoons or pots and pans, a steel oil drum as an actual drum. Turn a dandelion into an oboe, an elderberry into a flute.

Or make music the simple way: sing. Singing increases circulation and promotes deep breathing, both known to reduce stress, and singing makes people happy, especially in a group. Scientists posit that music is linked to group selection or cognitive development or cultural evolution, but we don't know how and we don't know why.

We just love to listen. So someone's got to play and sing.

———◆—◆———

65

NEGOTIATING

YOU MAY HAVE TO RESOLVE A CONTRACT or a border dispute. You may have to bargain for resources: how much food or water or firewood you'll use. Whatever you negotiate, know where you stand and what you want. Be willing to compromise but not to overaccommodate. When you sit down to talk, set ground rules, find common values, and brainstorm for solutions. If you reach an impasse, take a break. Then start again.

Never, ever give up. What's the opposite of negotiating? Bullying? Vying for domination? Waging war? Talking it over makes a lot more sense.

—————◆ ◆ ◆—————

66

PATCHING

ALLITERATION MAY HAVE KEPT IT OUT OF THE MOTTO "reduce, reuse, and recycle," but patching is an excellent way to do all three at once. You can patch clothes with scraps, packs with jackets, bicycle tubes with sneaker soles. You can patch roads with rocks and trails with cedar puncheon. Finding patch material, as any quilt maker will tell you, is half the fun.

Patching can heal as well. You can patch an injured eye against overuse or a burn against drying out. You can patch a friendship with kindness, an alliance with compromise, a marriage with forgiveness. (See also: *Mending*.)

67

PLANTING NATIVES

PLANT NATIVES — trees, shrubs, perennials — to create habitat for hummingbirds, butterflies, bees, or small mammals. Plant natives to preserve biodiversity. Plant natives because the flip side can be dangerous: plant a nonnative and who knows what havoc it might wreak? Tamarisk planted with the best intentions, as erosion control, now lines every waterway in the Southwest. Kudzu devours whole houses in the South. Purple loosestrife engulfs meadows in the Northeast.

If for no other reason, plant natives because they're easy. They're less susceptible to disease than nonnatives; they require less water and fertilizer and pruning. They're already adapted.

———◆◆◆———

68

PLANTING TREES

IN THE BACKYARD, IN THE PARK, along the road, or in a vacant lot. Plant trees for the environment, to process CO_2. Plant fruit and nut trees for food, pine and fir for lumber. Plant oak for firewood and alder for furniture (or vice versa).

Plant for yourself or the next generation. Plant in excess. Harvest in moderation. Plant for shade and shelter from the wind. Know the best species for the climate, for the location. Watch for roots in the drain field or leaners too close to the house. Plant in late summer or early fall: the seedling will spring to life in spring. Water well and often, and mulch heavily.

To grow an oak: collect green acorns, float the batch in water and keep the ones that sink, refrigerate in a ziplock bag with damp soil until germination (to mimic the dormancy of nature, usually about two months); plant in a pot, then in the ground. The same process works for growing pinyons (from pine nuts), only without the need for refrigeration: harvest, test, pot, then plant. *Voilà.*

69

PORCH SITTING

YOU CAN SIT ON THE PORCH ANYTIME, but late afternoon is best, near sunset on a summer day. Bring something to read, or not, because reading is about thinking and porch sitting is about not thinking. Porch sitting is about not doing anything except noticing the way the light filters through the cottonwoods or how raindrops bounce off the dusty earth.

When you're sitting on the porch, you are public property. Neighbors may wander by to say hello and discuss the weather or a party-in-planning or what a nice evening it is. If you're lucky, someone will join you.

Great ideas start on the porch. Great friendships, too. It used to be only smokers got this privilege, the excuse to go outside for ten minutes at a time with no purpose at all. But anyone can do it. Anytime.

◆ ◆ ◆

70

POTTERY MAKING

WHOEVER DISCOVERED POTTERY must've been delighted. All
you need is clay and fire! If ready-made clay isn't available
at the local crafts store, you can prospect for platelets with
a jeweler's loupe. Mix and match your minerals — kaolin-
ite, chlorite, illite, montmorillonite, bentonite — for elas-
ticity and hardness, from earthenware to stoneware to
porcelain.

Hard clay is, actually, hard to extract. Try a road cut unless
you have a blaster's license. Bring a bucket and dust mask.
Process clay by drying it in the sun, then pounding it to
powder and sifting it. If your product is lousy, you can add
water and store it underground to ferment.

Then comes the fun: make plates and bowls and mugs,
pitchers and urns and vases. Work by hand at first — try
a pinch pot or coils — then move up to throwing clay on a
foot-powered wheel. Fire your wares in a pit of coals covered
in sawdust, covered with yet more firewood. The bigger the
fire, the better. Invite your friends. When you extract your
creations, pour milk over them to create a glaze.

◆ ◆ ◆

71
READING

READ SIGNS, READ HOW-TO GUIDES, read great literature, read the Bible, read to connect with the past and to imagine the future. Read for pleasure and for the excuse to sit still. Read recipes for sustenance, obituaries for perspective, almanacs for minutiae.

Some people like to name one book they couldn't live without on a desert island: *War and Peace* for quantity, Emily Dickinson for delight, Shakespeare for drama, Harry Potter books for rereadability, Stephen King to get scared-as-heck around the campfire.

Why choose one? Start your library early. Add to it often. Guard it with your life. Avoid the fate of Alexandria: the greatest library in history didn't burn once but several times, by will and by accident. (See also: *Fire Fighting*.)

72
REVISING

TODAY WE REVISE TEXTBOOKS, software, political campaigns. In a changed world, we'll have to revise our plans, our expectations, our methods. By definition, revising means making changes to correct or improve upon, but it also requires stepping back, reassessing, sometimes asking for help.

Re-vision: seeing things anew. The best craftspeople are those who don't mind changing their minds. Ditto for the best parents. Maybe the job doesn't call for tile; maybe wood works better. Maybe you don't need a paragraph, just a sentence. Maybe the curfew is a little strict, or not strict enough.

It's easy to call this skill flexibility, but it's more than that. Revising isn't the willingness to change, but the doing of it.

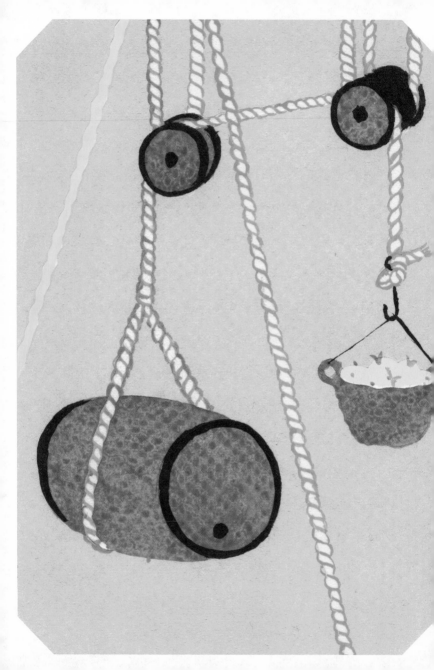

73

RIGGING

MECHANICAL ADVANTAGE DOESN'T REQUIRE FUEL. A pulley or block and tackle magnifies force, so you can lift heavier loads with less force. Friction aside, the more pulleys, the more pull. No crane or excavator needed. A grip hoist or come-along requires no energy source but your own.

Think about your angles: the more direct the pull, the greater the advantage. But think about safety, too. A straight pull might be easier but puts you in danger if a rope or cable snaps or a load shifts unexpectedly. Find a safe place to anchor, attach a choker, pull up the slack, and watch things move. You'll appreciate the addictive magic of this skill when you've lifted a thousand-pound footbridge into place all by yourself. (See also: *Using Leverage.*)

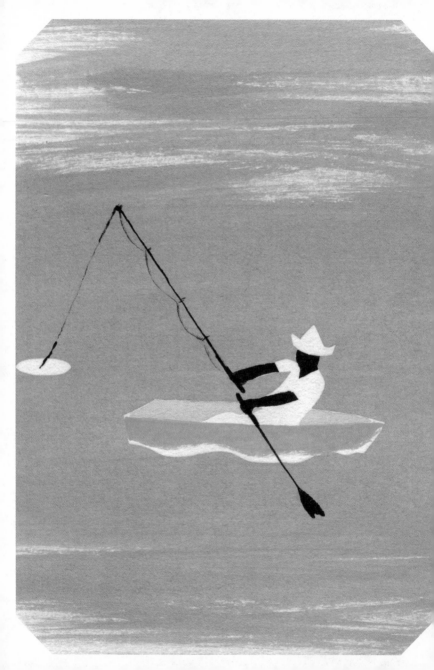

74

ROWING & PADDLING

WHEN YOU ROW, YOUR OARS ARE LOCKED to the gunwales or outriggers. You move them in tandem, usually facing the stern to maximize your stroke. (Picture the crew teams on the Charles River.) Though occasionally you may face forward to navigate rapids. (Picture wooden dories on the Colorado River in the Grand Canyon.)

To get started, grasp the oars gently and practice your terms: the catch and extraction, the stroke and recovery. Breathe with the stroke or breathe in recovery, but breathe regularly, and relax.

When you paddle, your paddle is free. You can have a single-blade paddle for a canoe or a double-blade paddle for a kayak, but either way, it will not be fixed. In a canoe, learn the J-stroke and the draw stroke. In a kayak, learn the power and the sweep strokes.

For all of the above: Learn what to do if you capsize. Keep an eye on the wind and tides and water temperature. Bring a friend and a fishing rod. Or bring a week's worth of food.

Don't forget a life jacket!

75
SAILING

FROM ANCIENT EGYPT TO THE AMERICA'S CUP, sailing has proved the most efficient nonmotorized transport humans have ever known. Faster than a hot-air balloon, less taxing than a bicycle, more versatile than a sled or skis. You can circumnavigate the globe on wind alone.

Of course, it requires skill and knowledge — not to mention a brand-new vocabulary — to man the rudder, tack and jibe, reef the sail and rake the mast, to captain a schooner, a ketch, a yawl, or a Bermuda sloop. Take a class to learn the basics, many of which could save your life: boat handling, knot tying and splicing, sail trim, seamanship, marine navigation, collision avoidance, boat maintenance, and emergency repair. Again, don't forget the life jacket!

For inspiration, try Joshua Slocum's *Sailing Alone around the World* (1900), a kind of watery *Walden*. For direction, pick up a sailing manual.

In the end, it's not all efficiency and safety. On a sunny afternoon, you coax friends from dry land, sail across the cove, and return them to shore windblown and ecstatic. Now they're hooked. Fair warning: sailing is highly addictive.

76

SEED COLLECTING

COLLECT SEEDS ALONG ROADS OR TRAILS, from neglected gardens, well-tended parks, and abandoned fields. Collect where plants are threatened by development or neglect or climate change. Plant them where they'll flourish. Wildflowers are ever-popular, but don't forget native grasses and shrubs. Remember to use a guidebook and key your plants carefully. (See also: *Latin Names.*)

Avoid collecting endangered species or from small plant populations or private property. Many species are hard to recognize when they're not flowering, so mark them in bloom — with flagging tape or a scrap of rag or a rock cairn — to find them later. Store your seeds someplace cool (less than 50 degrees) and dry (humidity less than 50 percent). If your seeds are too wet, decaying, or insect damaged, they can ruin all the rest of your collection one-bad-apple style, so be vigilant.

Many native seeds require cold/moist treatment, ingestion by birds or animals, or scarifying (breaking of seed coat before germination). These you can sometimes approximate. A coffee grinder, for example, scarifies effectively. Swap information and seeds with friends and with the local seed bank. (See also: *Seed Saving.*)

◆ ◆

77

SEED SAVING

WHAT WOULD WE DO WITHOUT STACKS of garden catalogs in winter? Save our seeds, of course! Saving seeds ensures we grow plants best acclimated to where we live; it's as local as local can get. But there are a few ground rules.

Avoid hybrids since, like mules, they cannot reproduce. Avoid, too, plants whose flowers can be cross-pollinated, like eggplants and peppers and squashes. Focus when possible on heirloom varieties, older and less familiar strains, for diversity of species and flavor.

Tomatoes are self-pollinating, so they're a good place to start. Allow the fruit to ripen thoroughly on the vine, then spoon out the pulp with seeds and place it in a nonmetal container where the pulp and seed covering can ferment for about three days. Then rinse and rinse again in a bowl or basin until the clean seeds sink to the bottom. Dry, package, label, and date.

Store in a cool, dry location. Come spring, try to remember where that was.

◆ ◆ ◆

78

SHARPENING

DEF. 1. Sharpening a blade

For a knife, use a stone or a strop. For a saw, you'll need a file, set, and gauge. For a scythe, you'll need a whetstone. Take it slow. Time spent sharpening is time saved working.

Forest Service trail crews who use crosscut saws in federally designated wilderness areas know that non-power saws can be remarkably effective. Not chainsaw-fast, but not ax-slow either. Problem is, since anyone with some stamina can use one, anyone can ruin one by dragging it through dirt or over rocks. Good crosscut saws haven't been made for 70 years, so sharpening will be in high demand.

DEF. 2. Sharpening awareness

Awareness of other people leads to empathy and listening skills, which can make you a good negotiator, teacher, or leader. Awareness of the environment allows you to notice sights, sounds, smells, temperature, and sometimes danger. Hunters must be sharply aware of movement, subtle noises, changing patterns of behavior. Ditto for parents. Awareness is the seed of both insight and action. Keep yours sharp.

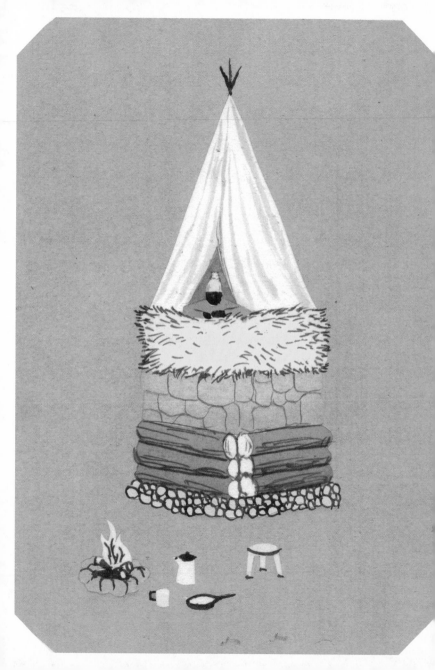

79

SHELTER BUILDING

USE WOOD OR STONE, FABRIC OR MUD, cedar bark as Pacific Northwest natives do, or ice like the Inuit. Use logs or hay bales or salvaged steel. Remember the lesson of the Three Little Pigs — make it sturdy — but consider, too, how long you plan to stay. A week or two? Try a canvas tarp or thatched palm fronds or willows. Even for longer stays, who needs a trophy home when a treehouse might do?

Plan first. Is there room for a woodstove, capacity for plumbing, enough southern exposure for sunlight, enough pitch to the roofline for snow to slide off? Don't build so big as to be wasteful. Don't build too small either, because guests always arrive. (See also: *Houseguest Hosting.*)

◆ ◆ ◆

7 TENTS

From a rectangle of available cloth, canvas, or plastic you can erect many different shelters.

Each sketch shows an elevation along with a view of the material laid flat. Dashed lines indicate folds, dots indicate fasteners, and circles show a ring, needed for suspension or pole support.

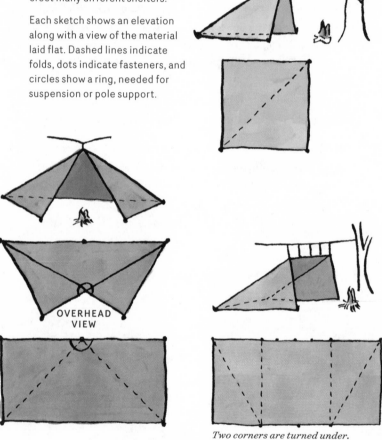

OVERHEAD VIEW

Two corners are turned under.

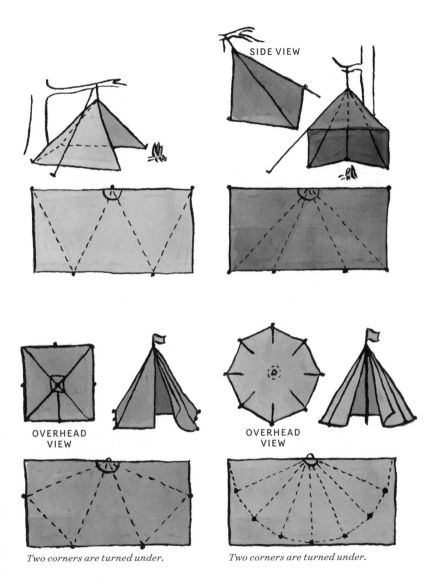

SIDE VIEW

OVERHEAD VIEW

OVERHEAD VIEW

Two corners are turned under.

Two corners are turned under.

80
SLEEPING

EARLY TO BED, LATE TO RISE, saves on lamp oil and firewood. Plus, sleeping saves energy, mostly your own, and keeps you healthy. Lack of sleep has been linked to heart attack, stroke, high blood pressure, obesity, psychiatric disorders, and poor quality of life. Sleeping is sustainable. It heals the body, encouraging muscle repair and hormone release, and recharges the brain, making you more resilient and more receptive to ideas.

If you have trouble getting to sleep, try yoga or meditation, warm milk or melatonin, mellow music or a not-too-exciting book. Why wait for the power reserves to run dry? Start now and get a jump on the future.

———◆◆◆———

81

SNOWSHOE CRAFTING

SEVERAL THOUSAND YEARS AGO people began to design snowshoes that mimicked animal tracks. There's the beavertail style with a round nose and a long tail and the bearpaw style, short and wide. Native Americans built some models that were 7 feet (2 m) long to float on deep powder.

Use ash and cowhide, or basswood and waxed thread, or salvaged aluminum tubing and nylon webbing. Steam the wood to bend it. Lace the sides together as if stringing a tennis racket, but with a hole in the middle so the foot can flex while the snowshoe stays level. If you live up north, make several pair.

82

SPINNING

TO MAKE YARN OR THREAD, you can spin silk or cotton, flax or hemp. Most people start with wool — raw and uncombed, oily and pungent with lanolin — or roving, cleaned and combed to align the fibers. You can use a drop spindle, a simple, toplike contraption that works by gravity, or a spinning wheel, treadle-powered and elegant. (Rumpelstiltskin used one; so did Gandhi.)

Draw out the wool fleece gently, a little at a time, until your bobbin fills. Transfer the yarn via a lazy kate (a bobbin holder) onto a niddy noddy (a frame designed for the task) or a reel to create a skein of spun yarn that you can wash, hang to dry, and then roll into a ball.

Your first tries will be inconsistent — too thick here, too thin there — as you get used to the pat-your-head, rub-your-tummy coordination of feet and hands. Save your first ball of yarn, the advice goes, because you'll never get that delightful inconsistency again. Once you've got the touch, you don't lose it.

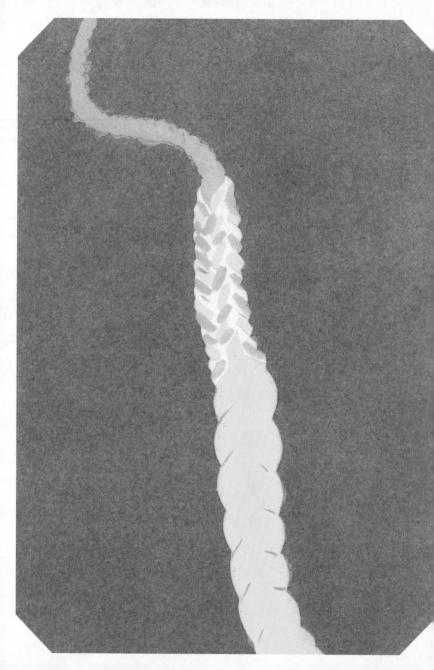

83

SPLICING

BRUMMEL SPLICE, EYE-SPLICE, back splice, chain splice. A splice is stronger than a knot, and it's made to last. You can splice rope for a sailboat, cable for a come-along, wire for conductivity.

If you don't have rope or cable or wire, you can make your own cordage. Use threads from a fraying bedsheet or strip the fibrous inner bark from cedar, poplar, willow, or elm, or collect the stems of milkweed, fireweed, or nettles. Twist the fibers between your fingers or roll them over a bare thigh. Twist one bundle one way until it kinks: now you've got two bundles. Keep on twisting the same way and they'll spiral around each other the opposite way until you've got 2-ply twine. Splice it together.

Next steps: *Knot Tying, Weaving, Rigging, Gliding, Sailing.*

84

SQUATTING

DEF. 1. *Sitting in a crouched position*

Who needs a lawn chair? Haunches are portable. In many cultures squatting is the norm, and it's much healthier, doctors tell us, than sitting in a chair. Squatting stretches your lower back, increases your balance, and keeps you supple, though it can be challenging at first if you've sat in a chair your whole life. Here's a hint: start by wearing shoes or boots with heels. Another benefit, common worldwide: squatting while defecating can eliminate elimination problems.

DEF. 2. *Staying on land or in an abandoned building not your own*

It's the wisdom of the hermit crab and the homeless, and it's the tried-and-true way to survive radical transition. Find a place and make it your own, but beware the wrath of the ostensible owner. Be prepared to move on.

85

STAYING HOME

STAY HOME AND SAVE FUEL AND ENERGY. Stay home to grow food and cook it, to build stuff and repair it. Stay home to raise animals and children or to care for aging parents. Stay home to read or play music or sit on the porch or talk to neighbors. Stay home to sleep. Nearly every skill comes down to this one, the one some people like to do least. If you can't hack it, see instead: *Finding Your Way.*

---◆◆◆---

86

STONEWORKING

NOWADAYS SOME MASONS use mortar, cement, and lime, which must be mined and shipped, but dry stonework — building with stacked interlocking stones — has been around forever, and the material is everywhere. There's limestone in Kentucky, granite in Scotland and New England, columnar basalt in Turkey, not to mention river rubble removed from fields in the Dakotas, piled high, awaiting a use. Stone cathedrals have stood for a thousand years, stone houses and bridges even longer.

For starters try a wall. The classic stone wall or fence or "dyke," as the Scots call it, has a base 28 inches at the bottom, 14 inches at the top, 52 inches high. Flatten the ground with a shovel, a rock bar, or a mattock. Then it's time for the stones. Choose them, sort them, shape them, and stack them. Taper toward the top.

You can take a class or work with a master, but at some point the secret is simple: one rock at a time.

◆ ◆ ◆

87

STORYTELLING

STORIES PASS TIME, offer moral lessons, and open up possibilities: what has yet to unfurl in the future or might've happened in the past. Storytelling is often the realm of the outsider, the prophet, the clown, or the priest since stories are how we make sense of things, especially the parts we don't understand. A woman in a garden with an apple and a snake. A coyote who steals fire. A former king pushing a boulder uphill, over and over, endlessly.

You can tell stories around a campfire, from a pulpit, on the page, in a song; and the more stories you tell, the better you get at it. Making up stories is a gift. Telling them is a gift. Listening to them is pure pleasure.

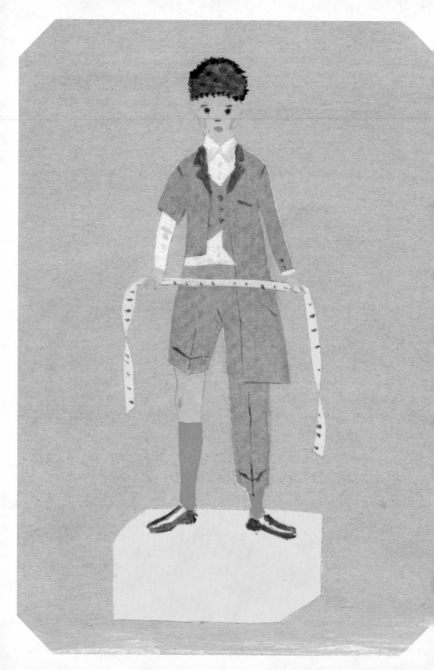

88

TAILORING

DEF. 1. Making a garment fit

If we're going to reuse clothes, we'll need to make them fit. Sew darts in the waistline or add elastic. Let down the hem for a growing kid. Cut off worn jeans to make shorts. For the more skilled: collect old sweaters and felt them into children's wear.

DEF. 2. Altering or adapting for a specific purpose

A job that used to require a backhoe can be tailored to shovel size. A house too big to heat through can be tailored by shutting off a room.

Expectations will be tailored all the time. Downsized, yes: adventurous spirits may not flit off to Antarctica or the Galápagos. But ratcheted up, too: a 15-year-old can do a lot more work than she may think. Ditto for senior citizens. Vacations can be tailored: a long afternoon at the lake can be as refreshing as a trip to Maui. Pull out that old pair of swim trunks, tailored now to fit right.

◆ ◆

89

TANNING

DID YOU KNOW THAT AN ANIMAL contains exactly the amount of brain needed to tan its own hide? True. A friend's boyfriend once tanned a deer hide he'd soaked with brains, hung on a clothesline in a chilly basement, and repeatedly stroked with a wooden oar. The room stank, but the leather was the softest you'll ever feel.

Want to try?

Start by laying the fresh hide flat and covering it with salt (plain or pickling, noniodized) until it dries to a crisp. Soak it in water for a day or two, then tack it to a stretcher and begin to apply the tanning solution. If you don't use the brains, you'll need to use a recipe that includes bran flakes, baking soda, and, most crucially, battery acid. No kidding.

(See also: *Disposing of Trash.*)

90

TAPPING

DEF. 1. *Tapping a maple for syrup*

Pick a maple, any maple. Sap surges when late-winter nights are below freezing and days above 40°F. Head out just before a major weather change or on a warm afternoon after a cold night. Drill a hole upward at an angle, and place your tap. Taps, called "spiles," are pegs made of plastic or iron or bamboo or hollowed-out wood. Hang a bucket or a milk jug to collect the sap. Next you'll boil it down and boil it down and boil it down (best done outdoors). You may get 1 quart from 10 gallons.

Note: Tap with care. Not too many trees, not too close together. No more than one tap per foot of tree diameter at breast height. The hole will take one to three years to heal.

DEF. 2. *Tapping a person for duty*

Call it delegating. Call it leadership. Someone has to recognize talent, divvy up the tasks, put the slackers to work. Someone has to keep an eye out for untapped potential. Then tap it.

DEF. 3. *Tap dancing*

Why not?

91

TENDING

DEF. 1. Managing wild resources

Somewhere between the hunter-gatherers and the farmers
lies another kind of culture: those who tend. These indigenous peoples have, for generations, tended wild landscapes
by altering them to meet their needs for food, clothing,
and shelter. They might prune or coppice willows to grow
more shoots for basketry, or start low-intensity fires to
clear open space for ungulates or to encourage ponderosa
pines to reproduce. "Traditional ecological knowledge," it's
called, and it's one model to follow for a sustainable future:
to use what's wild without stripping it of wildness.

DEF. 2. Paying attention, applying oneself, serving

Tend a garden. Tend your children. Tend to your work, your
health, your art, your spiritual well-being.

◆ ◆

92

TINKERING

DEF. 1. Mending with metal

A tinker used to be an itinerant tinsmith, a traveling mender of household items, especially with tin, but using all kinds of metal. You could do worse, in an unpredictable future, than to travel and mend with metal: trash can lids, silverware, or discarded tin cans could be used to repair cookware or yard tools, clocks or carts, lamps or candleholders. Or even the proverbial "tinker's wad" or "tinker's dam" — an insignificant, worthless piece of, well, anything — could patch a hole when soldered into place.

DEF. 2. Making hasty repairs

Not all repairs are perfect or permanent. To tinker requires ingenuity and creativity, the ability to make use of whatever is at hand, or to reinvent what doesn't work quite right. If you don't tinker, you'll likely depend on someone who does.

DEF. 3. Puttering

How else is a true tinker's ingenuity groomed? (See also: *Daydreaming.*)

93

USING LEVERAGE

SAY YOU NEED TO REMOVE LUG NUTS or lag screws or a section of threaded pipe but you can't budge the wrench. A cheater bar, a piece of pipe, short or long, slipped over the handle gives you a little leverage and solves the problem in a jiffy. Then there are the bigger issues. To move a boulder off a road or trail, cut a green sapling, prop it on a smaller rock (the fulcrum), and lever away. It works every time.

Note: The problem with leverage arises when it makes you too powerful, as when the sapling snaps or the political landscape shifts or the finance major starts fooling with derivatives. Then there's trouble. Using leverage is great — until it's not.

94

WALKING

IT'S A GOOD WAY TO GET PLACES — no equipment needed — and it's good for your health. Walking briskly for exercise lowers your risk of developing heart disease, diabetes, and stroke, and it makes your bones stronger.

Walking regularly also puts you in very fine company, especially if you have a literary bent. Louisa May Alcott walked 10 miles a day. Henry David Thoreau famously claimed, "I cannot preserve my health and spirits, unless I spend four hours a day at least . . . sauntering through the woods."

With ambulation and improved circulation, you might also find inspiration. As J. K. Rowling once said, "Nothing like a nighttime stroll to give you ideas."

◆◆

95

WATER COLLECTING

WE CAN DO EVERYTHING RIGHT — reuse greywater, figure out a way to desalinate, conserve, conserve, conserve — and still we may someday find ourselves without this vital resource. The first step will be to learn how to collect it.

Spend a week at wilderness survival training, and you might learn to hollow out a pithy alder log with a sharp rock to siphon up a puddle. Before drinking, boil the water with rocks heated in a fire. Switch out the rocks often. Move to the rural Southwest, and you might learn to channel rainwater from a roof to a barrel, enough to supply a household: laundry, showers, and all. Wherever you are, hoard buckets, bottles, and tarps (lots of tarps — liberate them from logjams at low water).

Even the strongest among us can survive for only a handful of days without water. Best to be prepared.

———◆◆◆———

96

WEARING CLOTHES

ON SURVIVAL-TYPE REALITY SHOWS on television, the contestants never wear clothes. Sure, they wear bathing suits, but that hardly counts. Clothes aren't just for fashion, they're for protection: from the weather (cold, rain, wind, and sun — what if we can no longer get SPF-50?) and especially from bugs. The threats from insect-borne disease — malaria, Lyme disease, West Nile virus, Rocky Mountain spotted fever — are real and ever-present.

And while the health effects of bug dope have been deemed negligible by experts, the danger to the environment is harder to gauge. Trace amounts of DEET are already ubiquitous in our streams and almost certainly in our drinking water.

So tuck your pant cuffs in your socks, wear a wide-brimmed hat, pull up your collar or drape a bandanna over your neck. Wearing clothes is cheaper, safer, and more effective than using chemicals . . . though probably not as good for Nielsen ratings.

◆ ◆

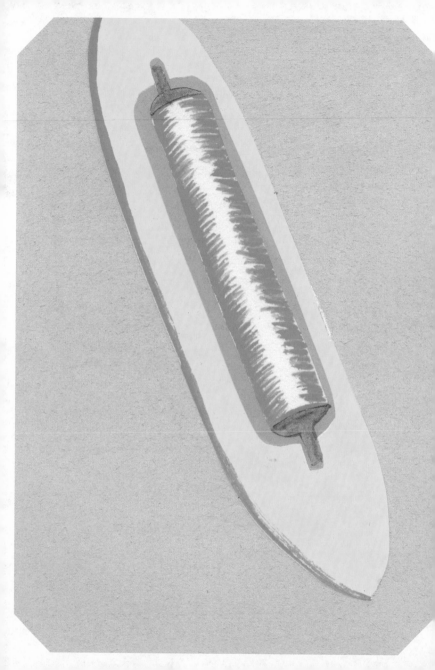

97

WEAVING

ALMOST AS ANCIENT AS HUMANITY, and as critical as any skill on the list, weaving arguably led to the development of agriculture and industry and even, eventually, to computer code. Weaving is also universal, practiced in cultures worldwide... even in preschools.

To weave fabric, you interlace the warp with the weft, winding your weft yarn onto a bobbin that fits a shuttle and inserting it over and under the warp threads. Start by making towels or placemats on a rigid heddle loom. Later you might progress to a foot-treadle floor loom, with four shafts or eight or even sixteen, to weave rugs or blankets or drapery.

Remember: the larger the loom, the more space you'll need. Luckily, weavers' guilds abound. Join one to share your passion, your knowledge, and a loom.

98

WELDING

TO REPAIR A BRIDGE, to design tools or hardware, to reuse broken machines, welding can be the key. (Note: Blacksmiths work from a single piece of metal and rely on fasteners, while welding causes coalescence, an actual bond.) Only problem is, for now at least, the art of joining two metal parts requires either electricity or pressurized gas, oxyacetylene. Metallurgy — hammering two forge-heated pieces of metal together with borax as flux — was the only process available until the 1800s, but even the most experienced blacksmiths find it difficult today.

Off-grid you can make do with a welder/generator combo or DC batteries and two coat hangers. Both techniques are tricky and imprecise.

The best advice: Start now, learn the standard way, and improvise later. Take a welding course at the local community college. Know your metals. Protect your eyes and skin. Hoard your flux wire. Hone your imagination. You'll know you've arrived when you can weld upside down.

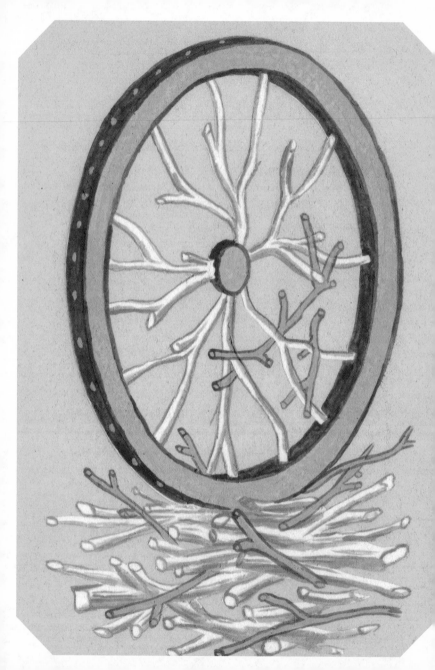

99

WHEEL BUILDING

MAYBE WE WON'T NEED TO REINVENT wheels for the future, but we'll have to rebuild them all the time. For bicycles, for wheelchairs, for wheelbarrows.

It may start out simply — salvage a tire and patch the tube — but soon there's more involved. Beat the rim back into shape or weld it. Find material for spokes (mix and match stainless, galvanized, carbon fiber, aluminum in a pinch) and cut them to fit. Calculate the number and tension them properly.

If all else fails, recruit the carpenter and blacksmith to bend sections of wood with an ax and adz into sections called "fellies" to be shod with strips of iron called "strakes" and nailed in place while the rim is hot and cooled fast. If it sounds hard, consider the alternative. (See also: *Walking.*)

———◆◆◆———

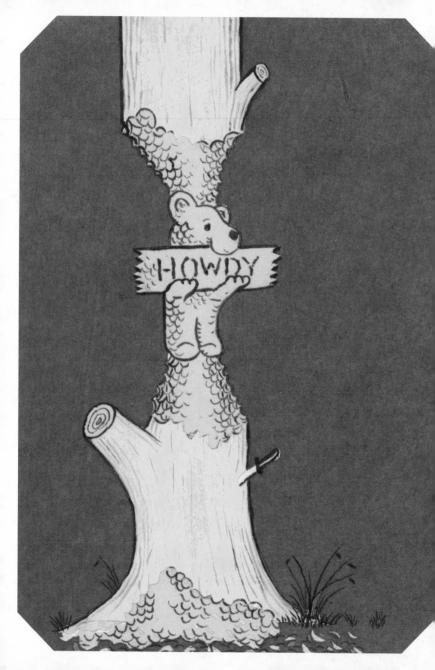

100

WHITTLING

DEF. 1. Carving shapes out of wood

Sharpen up your pocket knife and you can whittle a whistle, a spoon, or a letter opener. You can whittle a troll or a tiki. Basswood is best, but any soft wood will do. You'll need patience and a comfortable place to settle in, a rocking chair perhaps. (See also: *Porch Sitting.*)

DEF. 2. Reducing or eliminating gradually over time

Just think what might get whittled away while we whittle: debt, crime, pollution. The list could be endless.

———◆—◆—◆———

ACKNOWLEDGMENTS

This has been, fittingly, a communal project. My thanks to Jennifer Sahn and the good people at *Orion* magazine who published the short essay "10 Skills to Hone for a Post-Oil Future" that spawned this project and to the many readers who responded there with additional skills for the list. Thanks to Deb Burns at Storey Publishing for the vision for the longer project and for nurturing it into being. Thank you especially to friends and family who offered advice, explanations, demonstrations, time, and encouragement, including:

Pam Art

Mike and Nancy
  Barnhart

Dawn Barnicoat
  Emberson Bemiller

Deb Burns

Janet Buttenwieser and
  Matthew Wiley

Larry Cebula

Claudia and Chuck
  Charlton

Larry Cheek

Kelly Davio

Heather Durham

Sally Edgecombe

Claire Gebben

Iris Graville

Anne Penniston
  Grunsted

Stephanie Barbé
  Hammer

Melissa Hart

Jackie Haskins

Maria Hennessy

Lisa Hiley

Liseann Karandisecky

Kim and Walter
  Lundstrom

Kristy MacWilliams

Carleen Madigan

Sean McHugh

Tess McHugh

Iris Moore

Alethea Morrison

Dan Mulcahy and Jim
  Parham

Christine Myers

Kathie Neff

Nancy Norton

Jeremiah O'Hagan

Karen Olson

Michael C. Payne

John Peck

Julie Ann Higgins
  Russell

Ilona Sherratt

Joe Spagna

Sue Spagna

Gwen Steege

Laurie Thompson

Kate Zylland

ANA MARIA SPAGNA is the author of *Potluck: Community on the Edge of Wilderness*. She lives in a remote community in the North Cascades of Washington State, accessible only by trail, boat, or float plane, and without telephone service of any kind. Among the 90 people in her small town, they have 97 of these 100 skills covered.

BRIAN CRONIN is originally from Dublin, Ireland. His work has been featured in a solo retrospective at the Irish Museum of Modern Art. A regular contributor to the *New York Times, The New Yorker, GQ,* and other publications, he now lives in Brooklyn. His best survival skill is making images and imagining beautiful interiors.